PERF

BEYOND

PRESSURE

The Keys to Realising

Your Potential

RICH HUDSON

To Lydia

Best wishes

A catalogue record for this book is available from the
British Library.

Cover design by *www.tealzebra.co.uk*

ISBN 978-1-9996335-1-6

www.rdh00.co.uk
Twitter: @rhduson00

CONTENTS

PREFACE

Perform Beyond Pressure refers to performance and pressure in a sporting context, and often cricket, because this is the field that I work in as a coach and a managing director. However, the principles in the book are equally applicable to other fields of endeavour. There are many aspects of life that might benefit from also being considered a game. Therefore, the book looks to benefit both performance and enjoyment, on and off the field and in and out of the workplace.

The book is a distillation and combination of the most helpful things that I have learned and my own insights about the topics. This is shared within the 28,000 words that follow, along with questions to stimulate your own reflections and insights. What is contained within this book might be considered psychology, philosophy or spirituality. However, above all else, it is what I have found to be most simple and impactful. I hope that you find the same.

INTRODUCTION

"What You See, Is What You Get."

The purpose of *Perform Beyond Pressure* is to change how you see performance, pressure and yourself. Because when what you see changes, what you get changes.

Perform Beyond Pressure explains how you can become the very best that you can be while still retaining your sanity and enjoyment of the game. It will enable you to see, with clarity, how to:

- Adapt to the situations that you face

- Play the game, one moment at a time

- Move beyond what gets in your way

- Maintain your love of the game

It does not tell you what to think or how you should feel. *Perform Beyond Pressure* explains how your experience of pressure and performance works. It will provide you with a clear understanding of the game and what you need to know to play it effectively. It considers what the game means to you and how that can influence your sense of identity. This knowledge will allow you to plot a course that is unique and authentic to you.

To *Perform Beyond Pressure*, there are three keys:

1) Know Yourself

2) Understand The Game

3) Play Your Game

Throughout the book, 'The Game' refers to the sport that you play, but it could apply equally to other pursuits and careers. 'Your Game' is your way of playing 'The Game' and a 'Match' is used to describe a contest between two opponents.

You play the game the way that you do because of how you understand it. It is what you see and realise for yourself that matters. Therefore, do not take anything in *Perform Beyond Pressure* as gospel. Compare it with your own direct experience. Consider what makes sense to you, decide on what is going to help you and use that. Test it out for yourself so that you make your own trail in the game.

Perform Beyond Pressure provides the underpinning

knowledge about yourself and the game, which will then create your own insights. These insights will shift your perspective, enable you to realise your potential and enhance your experience for the better, both on and off the field.

PERFORM

"A journey of a thousand miles begins with a single step"

Lao Tzu

Performance is the fusion of skill and game awareness. There is *the* game - with its own rules, key principles of how to play and measures of success - and *your* game - your unique method of playing, ability to adapt and capacity to allow performance to flow.

Your level of performance will always be evaluated externally through results, awards, prize money, status and people's opinions. Performance is also assessed by you, internally, through your own perceptions of success and enjoyment.

When performance is measured by the concepts of success or failure, it is easy to innocently adopt other people's views on what success is. *Perform Beyond Pressure* will help you to achieve the results that you are capable of without losing sight of yourself. This will enable you to pursue what you enjoy doing and be yourself, ensuring that achievement does not come at the cost of inner fulfilment.

Once you are sufficiently skilled at the game, the biggest barrier to performance is your own mind. Overthinking, and being consumed within your emotions, prevents you from being able to produce your best. However, if you understand the nature of your inner experience then thoughts, feelings and perceptions no longer throw you off track. When you understand yourself, you are not weighed down by false ideas that create, and attempt to sustain, an illusory self-image. With this understanding, you become comfortable feeling uncomfortable and able to trust your instincts.

Performance is driven by learning - about the game, your way of playing it, the opponents and the challenges. It is about striving to 'master' the game on a continuous journey of learning, refining your craft and resilience. However, there is also a necessary *unlearning*. This happens as you let go of ideas that only get in your own way. By becoming aware of the underlying dynamic that has held you back from realising your potential, you can then move past it.

There are numerous factors in performance. When technical, tactical and physical ability is accounted for, the most valuable capacity is to always bring it back to what matters most: the present moment.

You can get consumed by everything that you need to do both on and off the field. However, you can only do one thing at a time. Everybody likes to feel in control. However, control does not lead to peak performance. The desire to be in control of everything stems from a fear of the unknown, and only distracts from what is the most important factor right now.

Play *this* ball. That is it. Be, here, now.

If you feel unsure or need a reminder, come back to this maxim. Play *this* ball. Wherever you are, whatever the next ball is, play it to the best of your ability. Leave the previous ball behind and do not worry about what the outcome of the match might be. Play what is right in front of you, in this moment.

The simple, uncomplicated nature of playing one ball at a time allows you to perform to your potential. As you intuitively become more attuned to what is required right now and how to do it, both your skill levels and tactical awareness instinctively rise both in matches and in practice. Inevitably, ability does matter when it comes to performance. If you have never played football before, being 'in the present moment' may not help much if Lionel Messi is in the opposing team. However, when you walk out on to the field, what matters most is only playing the game in front of you and not the story about it in your mind.

When a performer plays one ball at a time for long enough, it begins to feel as if they are 'in the zone'. It feels like you are both anticipating everything - all eventualities - and at the same time, anticipating nothing - by having no preconceived expectations. All you are doing is one thing at a time, irrespective of what has happened in the past or what might occur in the future. 'The zone' is the feeling that arises when someone fully realises that all that matters is *'Now'*.

Feeling under pressure *and* it negatively impacting your performance, is to be '*caught in thought'*. You get caught in anxious thoughts and feelings about performance resulting in you overlooking your capacity to play *this* ball. One insecure thought about the potential consequences then rolls into another. However, while these thoughts may feel uncomfortable, they are a temporary perception. They are not a prediction of the future, or an inhibitor of performance. That is unless you fall into the trap of believing this thinking and the notion that feeling this way can actually prevent you from playing your best.

You do not have to think that you can win. You only have to *play this ball*, no matter what you are thinking. Whether you feel good or bad, in rhythm or out of sync, simply play the next ball. To do this, you must understand the illusory and transient nature of thought. Consequently, thoughts and feelings do not grip you. You stay in the game and find out that anything is possible, despite what you might have thought. Before you know it, you are immersed in the game and how you feel has become an irrelevance. The game starts flowing and all you can do is go with it, as it comes, right now.

BEYOND

"Out beyond ideas of wrongdoing and rightdoing, there is a field. I'll meet you there."

Rumi

Going beyond is about looking deeper. Rather than scratching at the surface, be prepared to see things differently. Acknowledge that there might be a more efficient approach to performance. To go beyond pressure, you must first realise that something *beyond* your current perception might exist. From there you can go beyond a limited perspective to the wide-open possibilities of your potential.

For as long as you think that you must perform *under* pressure, you will be inhibited by it. Rather than seeing pressure as a weight bearing down on you, that you have to learn to cope with, the key lies in being able to go beyond it in such a way that pressure does not even appear to be pressure anymore.

The key to going beyond pressure is to understand it. There is little value in trying to cope with or fix pressure. As you understand pressure differently, your thinking automatically changes because your perspective already has.

Understanding underpins everything. Everyone's actions

are based on their understanding of how things work. If you understand how the game works, you will play it more skilfully. The more that you understand yourself, the more your abilities will shine through with greater clarity and ease.

This is not about mental techniques or coping strategies. At best, they have a placebo effect - a short-term benefit that wears off because your understanding is still the same as it always was. What really matters is how you relate to your internal and external experience. It is *understanding* that changes everything - a change in perspective that sticks because you now see *everything* differently.

Understanding is about seeing the truth or value in something for yourself, rather than it being another concept or idea that you have heard. There is no limit to the possible depths of understanding. Understanding strips away the noise that gets in the way of playing to your potential.

A real understanding of something - when you just get it, whether you can put words to it or not - occurs through natural shifts. Insights. They are the opposite of trying to solve a problem through mental struggle. Insights are as likely to occur when you are taking a walk or having a shower as when you actively try to work it out. Most people are so consumed by their own thinking - analysing, judging, comparing - that they have forgotten the power of having nothing on their minds. With less on your mind, there is more space for a fresh perspective to appear. When you insightfully see something for yourself, change happens instinctively.

Insight is learning and unlearning in equal measure. Learning something that takes you forward. Unlearning something that has inhibited you. When you let go of an unhelpful thought or belief the perceptions and behaviours that they caused begin to fall away naturally. The chances are that you will only realise how much your insights have shifted your perspective by looking back, from some time in the future, at how far you have come.

Perform Beyond Pressure asks you to be open to discovering a deeper understanding of yourself, your inner experience, how you view success, the game, and your game. A deeper understanding is realised through being open to *not knowing*. If you think that you have it figured out or that no other possibilities exist or that no further potential can be realised, you are then unable to learn or unlearn. With an openness you can embrace the opportunities that arise. You become more skilful, adaptable, comfortable in yourself *and* in feeling uncomfortable.

PRESSURE

"There is no pressure pre-existent in the world or inherently present in any given situation. The only pressure we can ever feel is 100 percent generated via Thought in our own mind."

Michael Nell

Pressure is a feeling. Feelings are made of thought. Thought and feeling are two sides of the same coin. You experience pressure at the same time as experiencing insecure thinking about what the event, and particularly the outcome, appears to mean. Feelings of pressure in performance are almost always related back to one of these elements:

- The level or standard of the game

- The perceived importance of the game

- Demands on you inside and outside the game

- The consequences of the result

- Expectations of others

- Comparison to others

Here is the critical point - it is not actually what is happening 'out there' causing your feelings of pressure. It is your beliefs, expectations and thinking *about* these elements. Pressure is a story that you have taken to be real - a story that says that you *need* the game to go a certain way.

Pressure is not the level, standard or importance of the game. Pressure is not the demands on you inside and outside of the game. Pressure is not the expectations of, or comparison to, others.

Pressure looks that way because that it is how it appears within your thinking. Each of these elements have their own challenges that you need to navigate. However, they are all inherently neutral constructs. They have no power on their own to make you feel under pressure or to create any other feeling for that matter.

If you believe that certain matches, situations or people can create feelings of pressure then you will do more thinking about them. It is *that* thinking that creates anxious feelings. To go beyond pressure, you do not have to try to change the way that you think. When you understand where pressure *does not* come from, your thoughts and sense of perspective change automatically.

The nature of thought is that it fluctuates. There will always be ups *and* downs in your psychological experience. Because of this natural rise and fall of psychological weather it is natural to feel pressure from time to time. Everyone will experience pressure sometimes, just as everyone will experience every other When you know that this is how the inner experience works, pressure will no longer inhibit you.

Without this understanding, you can experience an unnecessary amount of pressure. This can feel like you are carrying a weight on your shoulders and is probably why performing *under* pressure is talked about so often.

There is one reason why you experience this weight of pressure: Misunderstanding.

Over time you collect ideas and beliefs about how the game works, and what you think you must do to succeed or prove yourself. Beliefs are thoughts that you have held onto for so long that they form your worldview. When you take these expectations about how things should go seriously, believing them to be a true, fixed reality, they create unnecessary amounts of pressure or anxiety about performance, as you seek to live up to them.

There is one solution to going beyond pressure: Understanding.

Understand yourself, the game and your game. This will provide greater clarity on everything that it takes to realise your potential. Pressure will no longer inhibit you. You will see it for what it is and know that you are always far more capable of performing than you might have thought.

KEY #1 KNOW YOURSELF

- **Your Own Path**

- **Ebb and Flow**

- **Thought**

- **Ego and Identity**

- **Awareness**

"When you know yourself and your opponent, you will win every time. When you know yourself but not your opponent, you will win one and lose one. However, when you do not know yourself or your opponent, you will be imperilled every time."

Sun Tzu

YOUR OWN PATH

"The thing that is really hard, and really amazing, is giving up being perfect and beginning the work of becoming yourself."

Anna Quindlen

Realising your potential requires taking your own path. Taking your own path is the commitment to always going beyond where you are. There are always two games taking place – the one out on the field and the inner game within your mind. Your own path requires undertaking both the discovery of your capabilities, and the exploration of your inner experience. It asks you to reflect on what happens and look beyond your perceptions and sense of identity, to make sense of the game for yourself.

For many, pressure gets in the way of their true potential. To go beyond pressure, you must go back to the very start - understanding yourself and your inner experience. This is the foundation. Consider *who* you are, *why* you are playing and *what* success looks like for you. If you do not, then you might find that not even the greatest achievement in the world will fulfil you in the way that you hoped that it might.

Others might expect you to fit their expectations, but what do *you* want and how do you want to go about it?

In the pursuit of performance, and through life, everybody accumulates layer upon layer of beliefs and experience. However, what you might need most is to strip away some of the labels and expectations so that you can be yourself again.

Once people see the nature of their inner experience, they react less to it. They see things as they are, unclouded by perception. They become more relaxed, more effective and increasingly efficient as a result. With your foundations re-established, an inner space, quiet and clarity reappear. You can play the game with freedom and be comfortable in yourself.

Everybody who plays the game goes on a journey within it. To improve, you must learn. You have to succeed, and fail, and take what you can from both experiences. Learning from others can be quicker and easier than a slower process of working it out for yourself. However, a quicker and easier solution is not always the best one. Learning from others only has any relevance if you value your own direct experience even more. Otherwise, you are just being conditioned by someone else's beliefs.

As much as anyone else can know, and as helpful as they are trying to be, it is better to trust your instincts above those of any 'expert'. The best expert that you will ever find is your own instinct. Finding your own path means valuing your own intuition and decision making, even though you may not always get it right and will need to admit and adapt to that.

You have far more of the solutions than you might realise. As you grow older it becomes normal to lean on your analytical abilities to solve problems. However, an overuse of this capacity leads to stress and burnout. There is innate intelligence within you, beyond your capacity to analyse, judge and compare. Consider how you learned to walk - the instinctive intelligence within you that enabled you to go from crawling to striding with no intellectual analysis. Playing the game in your own way requires a faith in yourself, and life itself, that goes beyond your intellect and your sense of identity.

Trusting your own path is about exploring your game and discovering your fullest potential. In trying to find the best version of your game, you will end up finding the truest version of yourself.

"Deep within, waiting to be uncovered, is your wisdom. It exists beyond anything that you are thinking."

Dicken Bettinger

EBB AND FLOW

"Between the banks of pain and pleasure, the river of life flows. It is only when the mind refuses to flow with life, and gets stuck at the banks, that it becomes a problem."

Nisargadatta Maharaj

Everybody experiences a natural ebb and flow in the way that they feel. Thoughts, moods and emotions all appear then disappear. Confidence does not last. Pressure does not last. Calm does not last and stress does not last. Excitement does not last and nor does anxiety.

Everyone prefers a pleasant thought and feeling to a painful one but, ultimately, life is about experiencing the entire psychological spectrum. If you do not understand that, it can become a habit to try to avoid, or numb yourself to, certain feelings.

There is nothing wrong with any feeling. It is OK to not feel OK. It is OK to feel down, unsure or anxious. These are as essential an aspect of your experience as more pleasant emotions. Go 'inside' a feeling and see what it is made of. You will only find illusory energy, energised by beliefs. These beliefs are only thoughts that you have taken to be true. When you see that it is an illusion, you realise that you can go beyond it.

All feelings only make sense in relation to another. For example, joy is only meaningful in comparison to disappointment. There are no definitively negative emotions - e.g. channelled anger is often cited as a reason for a great performance. There are simply different understandings and interpretations of the emotions we experience. It is knowing this that liberates someone from the natural fluctuations of their inner experience.

"Every thought, every emotion is only a tourist... and I am not a hotel. Let them come and let them go." - Mooji

Thoughts come and go, even when you are not actively trying to think. Some thoughts feel more like *your* thinking. However, just as breath arises within you, rather than you consciously breathing it, thoughts naturally arise within consciousness and then fall away. New thoughts are always showing up, except for the times when you identify with, and hold on to, an old thought. All thoughts, all feelings, are temporary.

Moods rise and fall, just like the tides of the sea. When the tide goes out, you do not judge it for being low. You do not try to stop it. You understand that it is a natural process. When the tide is out, you see more of the beach.

It gives you a different perspective. Left to go out, the tide inevitably rises again. People's moods are no different.

As a child, thoughts, feelings and moods flowed through you. Watch how quickly any young child goes from having a tantrum to being utterly engaged in having fun, with seemingly so little reason for the occurrence or the change.

Nobody can control what their next thought or feeling is going to be. Nobody would choose to be angry or upset. The thought that says "I can control the way I think and feel" is as much of an inherently illusory and transient thought as any other. Fortunately, simply experiencing a feeling cannot cause your behaviour to change. You have to believe that thought and then act on it.

To go beyond pressure is to become OK with it. If pressure arises, it is OK. The more you try to control or change the feeling of pressure, the more thinking you do and so the more stressed you become. This resistance to how you are feeling is based on misunderstanding the nature of thought. The desire for control only creates more thinking, more anxiety and more misunderstanding.

If you try to forcefully control your experience, it will spin out of control sooner or later. Let it be as it is - you are still capable and the feeling will come, and it will go, on its own.

When you struggle it is not because your experience continually fluctuates, it is due to the belief that it should not. We are unwittingly conditioned from an early age that there is something wrong with feeling low. Or that we should pursue happiness on the assumption that happiness is 'out there' in the world and can be attained.

Problems arise if you attribute the cause of uncomfortable feelings to something other than a collection of thoughts and, instead, believe that it is a 'truth' rather than a perception. When this happens, you get lost in your inner experience. No longer able to see the situation clearly, this sense of being lost is reflected out into your external actions. This is why you often see players venting at umpires or getting distracted by the crowd to no benefit.

When you feel low, frustrated, nervous, anxious or under pressure, you can get completely caught up in that feeling. However, if you look, it is not only a feeling but also a guide. It is a guide to your current internal state rather than the outside world. As you become aware that there is always another way of seeing the situation, you make much more effective decisions. Instead of acting out in a low feeling, only to regret it later when you see things differently from another state of mind, you immediately have more perspective on a low feeling.

> *"In every area of life everyone is capable*
> *of seeing from a higher perspective than*
> *they do now. You are never stuck. You*
> *are simply limited by the level you are*
> *seeing from. Limitation is always illusion."*
> *- Sydney Banks*

It can become a habit to search for good feelings in achievements such as results and money or through other people. However, the nature of feelings is that they come, and they go. This is the case no matter how good you are and what you have achieved (or not). If you want to feel more confident, let go of the belief that says you need to achieve something to be happy. Without the beliefs about what you think you *need* to be OK, gratitude and optimism naturally emerge. This is not just when things are going well, but also when results are not going your way. You begin to see the positives and opportunities from even the most challenging of situations.

The more that someone knows how their inner experience of thoughts, feelings and perceptions works, the less they get caught up in thinking that does not serve them well. As your inner experience begins to flow more naturally, performance in the game begins to flow more instinctively.

THOUGHT

"I teach people to question their thinking, and this changes their world."

Byron Katle

A thought is a thought. Nothing more, nothing less, until you start connecting the dots with the next thought.

All thoughts and feelings are an energy passing through your experience. No thought has any inherent meaning or power to make you act in a certain way. It just provides a temporary perspective. Therefore, you can experience a thought and then act on it or not. Your relationship with your thinking can change - whether you take it seriously, follow it or let it go.

Every time that you have said, "That was better than I thought it was going to be" is an illustration that your thinking is illusory. Just because a thought paints a certain picture does not mean that is actually the way it is. It is for this reason that a batter can feel convinced that they will miss the ball, but then swing and strike it out of the sweet spot. The more that you know that this is possible, the more effective you become whether you are experiencing 'positive' or 'negative' thoughts.

Your inner experience of thoughts and feelings appears to be created from the 'outside-in' so that situations, people and results determine your perceptions and the way that you feel. However, this is not actually the case. You experience your thinking *about* situations from the inside-out. This explains why two people in the same situation can experience it very differently. On a rollercoaster, some people are likely to be extremely excited while others are very anxious or fearful. This demonstrates that an 'outside-in' perspective is an illusion. Even when it feels like a rollercoaster can create anxiety, it cannot.

Because you experience thoughts all day every day, you can begin to take them seriously. They appear to be so *real.* What starts as temporary, illusory energy can become completely compelling. When you believe your thinking, you are limited by the thoughts that occur to you. It creates a filter through which you see the world. What is happening is then filtered through the lens of what has happened in the past. Thought produces a reality that becomes your experience. While it appears that you have direct contact with the world, in truth what you have contact with are your thoughts about the world. Without this knowledge, you might start to believe that doubts and insecurity are not just thoughts, but their appearance must make you a doubtful and insecure person.

People are only restricted by their past, their personality and their beliefs to the degree that they are not aware that these are all connected to, and derived from, their current thinking. Your memories are experienced, and your concerns about the future are imagined, right now, through your thinking. This works the same way for everybody.

Thought is the primary source of problems, and knowing that is the cure. Any thought, regardless of its content, is no more or less important than any other thought. The content of a thought only becomes a problem when you forget that it is a thought. As you understand that, you stop believing thoughts simply because you have experienced them. You stop taking thoughts personally. They lose their grip on you and naturally pass through consciousness. You realise that whatever a thought says, you can still do the opposite.

Once you understand how your mind works from the inside-out, it shifts your experience of all sorts of events, situations, and people. Instead of trying to change your world so that you can feel better, you understand that without energising illusory thoughts, you are free to play the game. The less that you get tangled up in your thoughts, and the more that you see yourself as beyond what you think, the more that you can be yourself and perform to your potential.

EGO AND IDENTITY

"I went from thinking I could be an important person by winning things to realising that winning things doesn't make you important. I realised that, in fact, it's better to be no one. Because that is freedom. As soon as you have an identity, you have to work to keep it alive."

Jonny Wilkinson

Distinguish between who you really are and everything else. 'Everything else' comes in many forms; the person you are trying to be, your skills, relationships, possessions, achievements and status. Things that you have are not who you are. Even your personality is only how you appear to be and is far from the entirety of who you are.

People anxiously attempt to cling on to their achievements and possessions because they think that it is those things that make them who they are. They are afraid of losing because they think that if they lose a match or their status, they themselves will be diminished and somehow less of a person. The nature of everything is impermanence. None of those things are going to last forever. They will change - maybe for the better or maybe for the worse.

Everyone has an ego - a self-image. Ego is simply your beliefs about yourself - who you *think* that you are. Problems arise if you believe that those ideas are the totality of who you are and that you must live up to them at the expense of everything else. When this happens to an individual, it is often said that they have a 'big ego'.

If you identify with your ego (i.e. you think that it is who you are) then your focus is on proving yourself, trying to 'be somebody' and proving other people wrong. You will believe your thinking about yourself and try to live up to it. For some, this sense of self is not a hindrance to performance, it can feel beneficial. However, the ego is a burden even when it appears to help.

When you are attached to the ideas of the ego, you have no option but to perform *under* pressure. You have to perform under the weight of expectation that comes with trying to live up to this self-image. The ego is never satisfied. No matter what you achieve, your happiness will become dependent on the next goal or ambition. Then, when you get there, it attaches to the next. The ego plays an endless game of "I will be happy when...".

As you go through life, you collect ideas about who you are and what success is. Subsequently, all your thoughts and emotions stem from the self-image that these ideas then form. The more strongly that you become identified with your ego, the more you lose your perspective on life.

Many people spend their lives trying to live up to these ideas, not having realised that they were imagined in the first place.

There is no definition of yourself that can accurately convey the full truth of who you are. It is easy to limit yourself with labels - "I'm a sportsman", "a brother", "a mother", "rich", "poor", "relaxed", "intense" and you can go on and on. There is nothing wrong with a label on its own. However, even at its best, it is a narrow perspective of a person at one moment in time.

Every label that you attribute to yourself will disappear eventually. The greatest sportsperson on earth will, at some stage, have to deal with the reality that they are no longer the best. If they have identified with the label "I am the greatest", and believe that is really who they are, then dealing with their new reality is likely to be quite painful. They will mourn the death of the identity that existed in their mind, and which was reinforced by the behaviour of the people around them and society in general.

There was a time in our lives before we all took ourselves so seriously. This was before we believed our thinking about ourselves. When you see how you have become embroiled in a web of your own illusory thoughts and beliefs, your attachment to these ideas loosens. Without a self-image to live up to, there is nothing to prove.

In the absence of being taken in by insecure thoughts, you play the game for the pleasure of it. You find intrinsic satisfaction in your accomplishments, not caring so much about what others think. You recapture that deeper sense of fun, curiosity and humility that used to be so natural. Underneath all those layers of beliefs and thinking, lies a natural resilience, motivation, and confidence: You.

AWARENESS

"There is nothing more important to true growth than realising that you are not the voice of the mind - you are the one who hears it."

Michael A. Singer

Clarity comes from being aware of the ideas that make up your identity and who you think that you are. When you see some of these beliefs for what they are, they fall away naturally. As they do, you automatically become 'more comfortable in your own skin'. You become happier in yourself, because you stop trying to live up to your own or anyone else's expectations. You become more relaxed because you stop trying to prove yourself. Instead, you find a natural, deep inner drive that instinctively motivates you to realise your full potential.

You are not your self-image. The answer to who you are lies beyond that. There is a part of you - an awareness - that is the same now as it was five, ten or twenty years ago. This awareness has witnessed your body change and your life experiences unfold. It is where every thought and feeling arises and disappears. It was there before the doubts, judgments and comparisons seeped in and made themselves at home in your psyche. It lies beyond everything that it is possible to possess.

It is here that the innate well-being of every person lies, beyond the transient thoughts that can obscure it. When you know that this infinite awareness is the most fundamental aspect of you, you can always find your way back to it. Both yourself and the world around you continually change, but awareness does not. You can turn back within, to your fundamental nature and be yourself.

Instead of accumulating possessions and achievements to try to make yourself feel good, what if the answers to well-being lay within you?

This space of awareness is always OK, has always been there and always will be. When you do not feel connected to this infinite awareness, it is because you have thoughts, feelings and perceptions that are clouding that connection. This cloud can get pretty hazy at times. You experience psychological weather, just as in the natural world where all weather systems appear then dissipate on the canvas of the blue sky. The blue sky does not change, it is just temporarily covered up. Awareness is the deepest aspect of you. It is what the blue sky is to the weather.

"Successful mountain climbers know that they must spend at least as much time, if not more, in tending to their base camp as they do in climbing mountains, for their survival is dependent on it."
- Scott Peck

Our senses, designed for survival, ensure that we focus on looking outwards, at our lives and performances. However, this leads to an oversight of the existence of this natural space of awareness - the base camp within you. When your perspective is limited and there does not seem to be another way, it is because a layer - a belief, an expectation or a judgment - has got added on to what is naturally already there.

With a deeper understanding of yourself, you have a broader perspective on life. You see the bigger picture. You see that what hurts emotionally, at the time, may be the springboard for future growth, learning and development. You realise that setbacks and failures are an essential part of the journey, and not something to be feared or avoided.

You realise that you are, and forever will be, *enough* exactly as you are. This inner knowing allows you to just *be yourself.* When you are authentically being yourself, you will always have the confidence that you need. When you are trying to 'be somebody' (living up to your own or others' projections), insecurity rises up and covers the natural, intuitive confidence that you were born with.

As wonderful as having dreams and high aspirations is, it is important to consider that even fulfilling your dreams may not give you everything that your ego desires. The high of fulfilling a life-long ambition may only last an hour, a day, a month or even a year. Of course, this feeling is great and so enjoy it, let it sink in. However, ultimately, it is called a high for a reason. Your psychological experience will then turn back down, and the normal fluctuations of the human experience will resume. The power lies in looking beyond that. While your experience will always oscillate, your well-being lies at your core – within the infinite awareness - regardless of the temporary perceptions and sensations that you experience.

Be grounded so that you are fulfilled whether the high, or

the victory, does or does not come. Then, you can fully enjoy the moment, regardless of where you are or what the result may be. Avoid spending so long looking towards the future that success always appears to be at a distant point in time, rather than what you are doing right now.

Most people want to be successful because they think that success will bring them happiness. However, this *want* to be successful just leaves them feeling *wanting*, and no achievement ever satisfies the desire. Your results do not define you. They are only a concern to your self-image - the ideas about yourself that you hold. However, good and bad results are equally OK to the *real* you.

Happy people are grateful, but it is not because they are making an effort to feel that way. They just do not hold the belief that their existence should be any other way than how it is. In the absence of the belief that it should be "this way", they realise how grateful they are for what they have. This is because they are not attaching their happiness to something that they do not have.

The only place where you will find true fulfilment is

within, by fully knowing yourself, irrespective of what you do or do not achieve. Fulfilment only lies within the aspect of you that has never changed regardless of how much your life has changed. It is not reliant on anything. You can only find this out, and experience it, for yourself.

Once you know that happiness only exists inside, creating successful results 'outside' becomes more straightforward and more fun. It gives the courage to chase your dreams while knowing that there is nothing - on a fundamental level of fulfilment, peace and enjoyment - that the dream can provide that you do not have already.

PBP KEY #1 KNOW YOURSELF: SUMMARY

1. The most important expert that you will ever find is your own instincts.

2. Your experience is created within - it only *appears* to be determined by the outside (people, results and circumstances).

3. Thoughts are transient and illusory. You do not have to believe what you think. The more that you realise this, the more that unhelpful thoughts and habits naturally fall away.

4. There is an ebb and flow to your inner experience (consider your moods) just as there are natural changes in the outer world, such as the rise and fall of the tides and the changing of the weather.

5. It is OK to not feel OK. There is no need to resist low feelings.

6. You are not your ego. You are not your possessions or achievements. You do not have to prove yourself.

7. Results do not provide lasting happiness. Knowing this makes them easier and more fun to create.

8. The most fundamental aspect of you is awareness. It is what makes you conscious of everything that happens. It is here that you find your innate well-being.

9. Fulfilment is not something that you have to achieve; it is what you already are. When insecure thoughts are not clouding your perception then this becomes clear.

10. Be yourself.

KEY #2 UNDERSTAND THE GAME

- **It Is A Game**

- **Motivation and the Love of The Game**

- **The Big Moments**

- **The Demands**

- **The Opponent**

- **Obstacles Beyond the Opponent**

IT IS A GAME

"Like life, basketball is messy and unpredictable. It has its way with you, no matter how hard you try to control it. The trick is to experience each moment with a clear mind and open heart. When you do that, the game - and life - will take care of itself."

Phil Jackson

The most valuable thing to know about the game, is that it *is* a game. The longer that you have been playing, the easier it is to overlook this. It becomes a test or work or a career. However, when you began it was a game, and when you strip it back to basics, that is still true now.

The level of challenge, and the demands on you, will change. Your thinking about the game may have changed. However, it is still the same game with a bat and ball, or a ball and goalposts, that it always was.

The dictionary definition of a 'game' is "an entertaining activity or sport." The person who should be most entertained by your involvement in the game, is you. The top three synonyms for "entertaining" are "enjoyable", "interesting" and "engaging". These are the reasons why you started to play.

This is not to say that it is *just* a game. "It's *just* a game" is a defence mechanism, used when someone is concerned that defeat diminishes them (or more accurately, their self-image). Saying this underplays the immense power, value and meaning of games. To say that it is *just* a game is to suggest that games are not worthy of your commitment and full-out effort. Actually, the opposite is the truth. By striving for your best, you experience the fulfilment that comes with immersion in the game.

Performers who realise that it *is* a game play with a sense of freedom. They have a smile on their face simply because they are playing, irrelevant of the score on the board. They care about their performances but play without fear of the unknown. They are unburdened by thoughts about what might go wrong. They see opportunities where others perceive risks. They are not afraid to try things and see what happens. They explore what might be possible. They fail and still they keep coming back, because to play the game is fun. They make watching the game enjoyable.

You will win and you will lose. Success and failure both have the potential to limit your perspective and make you believe that the game is more complicated than it is. They challenge you to remember that the game is still a game despite the status, money or awards that may now be at stake. The opportunities to learn, and improve at playing the game, never stop coming. If you keep playing, anything might happen.

Everyone has different ideas about what success is.

Where did your ideas about success come from? How strongly do you hold on to those ideas?

To what extent do you derive your self-worth from the achievement of those ideas? Why?

Everyone is aiming for success, to play well and win. Without considering what you believe success to be and why you think it is important to strive towards that definition of it, you can become a prisoner of your thinking. It can create an obsessive *need* to win whereby it no longer feels like a game.

The belief that you need to be a success and that the only way to define success should be based entirely on winning matches or trophies, creates the feeling of pressure. However, success is a thought - an idea - and not something fixed or even true. Everyone's definition of success differs because everyone has different thinking.

There is no doubt that winning at the highest level requires a phenomenal amount of practice, conditioning, analysis and planning. All of these are necessary components to win. However, obsessing over winning is more likely to make you tense up on the field than it is to help you to achieve it. Knowing that your enjoyment of the game is not entirely reliant on winning provides the freedom to express yourself in the game.

When you know that it is a game and that, as much as you may want the result to go your way, you do not need to win then you are free - whether you win or lose. The attachment to the idea of winning, and what you think that it means, creates a sense of neediness and clinging to the outcome. This gets in your way far more than losing ever does.

The times when you suffer are when you forget that you are playing the game. If your self-image becomes attached to the outcome of what happens, it starts to feel that the game is, in fact, playing you. This is because you now feel reliant on the outcome. When there is a match, tournament, or contract at stake, these are all 'a play' within the game. 'A play' of winning the match, the tournament, another contract. When you know it is 'a play', it just becomes a game within the game. You can give it everything, knowing the result does not say anything about *you*.

Over time, you will look ahead to consider what might be possible and to set goals. The danger is that you forget both the simplicity and the meaning behind why you started playing in the first place. You can focus on the endgame so much that you overlook the value of the journey. You might end up just ticking off one goal after another without any lasting sense of fulfilment.

Goal setting can help you to make and measure progress, but your targets can also hold you back. You can easily end up anchoring yourself to something that is 'acceptable'. You become 'good enough' without ever finding out how great you could really be. Alternatively, you can set goals that are not currently achievable and then 'beat yourself up' for not reaching them. This will happen if you do not see goals for what they are - a thought about what could happen.

You do not know what your full potential is. Therefore, it

is impossible to set a goal for it. While goals are a part of the game, you do not have to define yourself by whether you achieve them or not. Do what makes sense to you - which may be setting yourself a goal, or it might not.

Consider what would be meaningful to you even if no one else would ever know. Goals are best achieved when you relax and enjoy what you are doing.

What might happen if your goal became to enjoy the game?

It becomes less of a goal and more of a way of being.

MOTIVATION AND THE LOVE OF THE GAME

"Somewhere behind the athlete you've become and the hours of practice and the coaches who have pushed you is a little girl who fell in love with the game and never looked back... play for her."

Mia Hamm

Love is not always the word that people want to hear when you are talking about performance. They want to hear about outcomes or, at the very least, the process. Yet, it is love that underpins all meaningful, sustainable, enjoyable performances.

You did not have to work hard to fall in the love with the game. It was effortless. Enjoying the game is completely natural. However, you will begin losing your bearings pretty quickly if you complicate your play with ideas about how you think your performances will define you.

There are many things that you can point to as to why people *enjoy* playing the game. These include success, their teammates, getting outdoors and being active. Sport is engaging because the challenges never cease. Through every stage of your journey every opponent, every environment and every situation all provide different tests. Each test is there to stretch you. For all your limits to be broken and then to be rebuilt stronger. Then to be broken again before being rebuilt once more.

Consider the feeling of striking a ball out of the sweet

spot. It is almost indescribable in its sheer, unlimited sense of freedom. That split second between you knowing exactly where the ball is headed, and everybody else realising, is a completely captivating element of sport. However, it is so fleeting a moment that it compels you to keep playing to experience it again.

Sport is meaningful because you are surrounded by people who care. Even individual sports are reliant on teams of people working together to support the performer who delivers the 'telling blows'. Beyond the 'inner circle' of the team, your family and your friends, the audiences and the media are all also connected to your story. Being a part of something bigger than yourself is empowering.

There is only *one* element to why people *love* playing the game, though. You might call this 'flow' or 'losing yourself' or a deep sense of connection. The disappearance of feeling self-conscious, as insecurities and problems fall away, leaves you completely absorbed in the game. Time seems to stand still, the game just flows and you begin to sense the enormous scope of your potential. That is what everybody loves above all else.

That is the experience everyone is looking for whenever they do anything - the games that you play are no different.

As you get better at the game, and progressively play at a higher and higher standard, it is possible to forget the simple and yet utterly engrossing initial experiences that had you hooked. Sooner or later you layer up this instinctive experience, and reason for playing, with stories. Stories about what you think that your performances say about you or can provide you with. If you identify with, and believe these stories, insecurity follows as you strive to live up to them. Simple, natural enjoyment gets clouded with thinking about results, fame, and fortune. This thinking eats away at the initial enjoyment until it no longer feels like play, it has become work.

The external reasons for playing the game, such as results, proving a point, earning money or gaining status, can all be enjoyable. However, they are nothing in comparison with playing for your own enjoyment. No matter what the reward, they are not the reason that you fell in love with playing the game in the first place. You will never be completely satisfied by an external reward. It is like a mirage on the horizon. Even with the biggest rewards, as soon as you get there, you will always experience a "What Next?"

When your main motivation is to *get* something, whether that is 'proving yourself' or gaining another external reward, it is likely that you will at times fall into the trap of 'wanting it too much'. You lose the sense of fun, and the capacity to overcome challenges and express yourself on the field that once came so naturally. This is because you are not playing the game simply because you love playing it and, instead, are trying to use it as a route to validate yourself. You have become lost in the game, rather than a player of it. The love of the game is not just a 'nice' saying, it is what creates a deeper drive to play and improve with a sense of freedom not restriction.

We are always being drawn by one of two forces: Love or Insecurity.

Do you love playing the game?
Do you want to keep getting better even when your results fluctuate?

Are you content, fulfilled *and* driven?

Is the game fun, as well as challenging?

Do you love finding out what is going to happen next?

Or are you using the game to try to prove yourself?

Are you afraid of what you might lose if you fail?

Are you afraid of not knowing who you are if you do not make it?

Do you think that if you achieve a certain level of success then everything will be OK, you will be happy and then you can relax?

Is playing a hard slog?

Do you spend your time contemplating other things that you could be doing?

The answers to these questions are a good indicator of the force that you are currently most drawn towards.

If external reasons become your primary motivator, your enthusiasm and desire to play and improve becomes flakier. You can lose motivation because you feel like a failure or you are not earning as much money as you wanted or because of other people's negative opinions about your performances. By believing ideas about what needs to happen for you to enjoy playing the game, you have given your enjoyment away to a story. If anyone tells you that your enjoyment depends on achieving whatever it is that they believe matters, you do not have to take those ideas seriously.

True enjoyment is not contingent on anything. Not winning nor receiving player of the match awards. Not selections, prize money or praise. These elements will come and go.

> *"I love this game more than anybody, so I'm not all of a sudden going to wake up and say I don't like it anymore. It's a lot of sacrifice, a lot of effort that I have to put in every day. But I enjoy that because what I get in return is moments like today with my team and my family. It's priceless really." - Roger Federer*

The love of the game does not mean that you will always *feel* as though you are loving it. Thoughts and feelings will continue to fluctuate. Even players at their peak will feel frustration or despair at times. What will be clear though is a deep pull back to the game. Not to prove yourself, but because the enjoyment of the game outweighs the inevitable ups and downs in your outcomes. True enjoyment comes only from the fact that you are playing.

If it only feels like you love the game when you get what you want, that is not a real love of it. That is insecurity, which only gives you a break when you have given the ego what it thinks that it wants (e.g. a win). However, losing is OK. It is an essential part of the game. Losing is sport's yin to the yang of winning. Winning would mean nothing without losing sometimes. It is not what you wanted; it is likely that it hurts. But that is OK isn't it? You are OK with not getting what you want, unless you believe that by not doing so, it somehow lessens who you are.

The game always has a new challenge to stretch you and a new set of scenarios to work out. It is being open to this, rather than looking at the past (results you have achieved before) or the future (hoping to get to a certain level), that makes playing the game continually engaging.

Winning and losing has always mattered, but when you

look back there was a time when just playing the game mattered even more. The best feeling in the game is being immersed in it. When you are completely in the moment, in the heat of battle, there is nothing else like it. That is why you play. Whether that is in the backyard, your club ground or on the biggest stage in front of 90,000 people. We are always at our best when we are doing what we love, simply because we love doing it.

External rewards can look after themselves and become a natural by-product of doing what you love. What you are looking for is far simpler than any reward; it is the connection, absorption, and presence that comes with *just playing.*

THE BIG MOMENTS

*"There is nothing either good or bad,
but thinking makes it so."*

William Shakespeare

It can be easy to assume that the higher the level of the competition, the more pressure that exists. That international sport is 'high pressure', and recreational sport is 'low pressure'.

There is more complexity playing at an elite level. The opponents are inevitably more skilled, although that is only relative to your own skill level. There might be more money at stake and more expectation from other people, with increased adulation if you succeed or more criticism if you lose. However, a more complex game against skilful performers does not equate to pressure, unless you believe that it does. People can feel pressure at every level. People can play with freedom at every level.

All the variables at every level - opponents, money, adulation, criticism - are inherently neutral. They are what they are. The extent to which they seem like a blessing or a curse is always a temporary, thought-created perception.

Performers may take themselves more seriously when playing at a higher level. This occurs when they identify their self-image as a 'high performer', and therefore derive their self-worth from their results. You do not have to carry this burden. When you know yourself, it is possible to approach even the highest level with a sense of fun and enjoyment. People worry that enjoyment will detract from the necessary commitment to developing their abilities. However, commitment and enjoyment go hand-in-hand when you take the game seriously, but not yourself.

Within a match it can be assumed that, as the situation becomes more difficult, the amount of pressure an individual will be feeling increases. We often hear commentators say, "They are piling on the pressure". This use of the word 'pressure' refers to the external situation of the match. However, it might also assume that as one side gains momentum in the balance of play, the challenge this poses will create an internal sense of pressure within individuals, which will lead to those players making mistakes.

A more difficult game or scenario can induce mistakes. That is common sense given that the game is a test of skill. However, any feelings of pressure or anxiety are not determined by the contest itself, the specific scenario or indeed any mistakes that have been made. An opponent is only going to be psychologically impacted by the match situation if they experience temporary, panicked thinking *and then* buy into it and believe it. This leaves them without the clarity to instinctively play the situation.

Learn to differentiate what is happening in the match from how you feel about it and, critically, from your capability to adapt and perform in the situation. As you become more aware that there is a distance between you and your thoughts, you find a greater perspective on what takes place within the game. This sense of perspective provides you with more options of how to approach the situation.

How important any game appears to be is a perception. You might think that a World Cup Final is a high-pressure game. However, you might see it differently. For example, you might see it as an amazing opportunity - a chance to express yourself on the biggest stage. Or you might see it as just another game. Alternatively, you might not think about it much at all - you will just go out there and play the game as it comes.

There are no high-pressure situations. There are situations and, at the same time, there are temporary perceptions and feelings about them. However, there is no causal connection between these two variables, despite how it can seem to all of us at times. Even a World Cup Final is only as big as you believe it to be.

When it feels like a situation is 'high pressure', this is an 'outside-in' illusion. When you know that 'outside-in illusions' exist, you begin to intuitively spot them as they appear in your mind. This causes the habit of perceiving matches to be 'high pressure' to fall away. Then the feeling of pressure no longer arises or, even if it does appear, you see the illusion for what it is. When you see an illusion, you are instinctively able to go beyond it. Therefore, it does not inhibit performance in the way that it might have done previously.

Some people treat every match in exactly the same way. Others play some matches as if they do not matter at all, and then try to raise their game for matches that they perceive to be the big occasion. These are all perceptions and are all perfectly OK in themselves. They are all different viewpoints, created through patterns of thinking.

If the game feels like a huge deal to you and you enjoy that and benefit from that, then there is nothing to do. Keep going. However, if you put some elements of the game on a pedestal (e.g. matches that you deem to be 'important') and view others as more inconsequential (e.g. training), it is easy to fall into the habit of playing with freedom in practice and then over-thinking in competitive matches. This happens because you practice with a lack of self-consciousness, relaxed by the belief that "this does not matter as much." Then you go into a competitive match with the belief that "this *does* matter", because "the results impact my self-image and my happiness". This causes you to tense up and attempt to over-control what is happening. You can end up with worse outcomes than you are capable of and little enjoyment.

It is simpler to treat all elements of the game in the same way. Then, everything becomes an opportunity to perform to your best, to challenge yourself and learn. It does not matter where, when or against whom. "Does it matter or not?" becomes an irrelevant question. Matches become training and training becomes matches. All aspects of the game merge into each other and you merge into the game.

Playing the 'big moments' becomes difficult when you become wrapped up in your thoughts about what this game means - i.e. what a big moment it is. You get concerned by what you think that this match might say about you - win or lose - and how others might react. If you believe that what happens determines who you are and how happy you can be, your thinking will fixate on the end result. This focus on the outcome causes you to play differently (e.g. more cautiously or more impatiently) because your attention is no longer on reading, and adapting to, the match as it unfolds.

It is likely that there will always be times when a situation feels like a 'big deal', despite how rationally you might try to think about it. The more often that you experience the same or a similar situation, the less it will bother you. You become desensitised to it through having been there before. However, there will always be new situations to encounter. This is why a deeper understanding of yourself, your inner experience and the inherent neutrality of the situation means that this perception will not be a burden on you if it arises.

In a tough situation, simply deal with what is right in front of you in that moment. Leave everything else. You can only do what you can do, right now. Whatever the action that is required, do it. Play one ball at a time. Repeat that process again and again, and so on. At the end of that simple process, you might look back and find a 'big' performance. Focus on what is required now and the result will take care of itself.

When you look back, the game is littered with times that you thought were a big deal at the time but now seem insignificant. This shows us that there are no inherently 'big' moments. Everything is neutral. Our thoughts and feelings in the moment create a perception of importance. It is absolutely OK for something to feel like a big deal, but it is helpful to know that it might not be.

Does this match/competition feel like a weight on your shoulders?

Do your beliefs about the pressure detract from dealing with the game simply as it is?

THE DEMANDS

"Don't sweat the small stuff... and it's all small stuff."

Richard Carlson

There is always more to performance than the matches, such as skills training, gym work, preparation, nutrition and recovery. There are also off-field elements that have the potential to either distract from, or enhance, on-field performance - contracts, the media, travel, social life, and relationships.

There are likely to be more of these off-field elements, and demands on, someone who is playing at a higher level. Whenever you are doing something for your living, and it takes up a large proportion of your time, there are inevitably more variables at play.

The key to simplifying what is happening 'out there' is to simplify what is happening 'in here'. The less you get caught in the flux of your thoughts and feelings, with ideas of proving yourself or beliefs about how things 'should be', the more clarity you have to deal with - and enjoy - all the variables that you contend with. As you do this, you will:

- Learn the elements that will enable you to realise your potential, and apply the appropriate time and attention to them

- Balance preparation with the elements outside of the game that are either necessary (contracts, the media, travel, diet) or enhance your life (relationships, social life, hobbies, developing skills and qualifications for life beyond the game)

- Remove any elements that do not enhance your performance or your life

Anything that begins as an off-field requirement can soon turn into feeling like a drain on motivation. Everything away from the game can begin to take over the things that got you playing in the first place. The same demands on a person can be seen from different perspectives. On the one hand, you see the positives - you are getting to live your dream, you are competing against the best, furthering your skills, creating the life that you want and seeing the world. On the other hand, you see the potential negatives - that you never relax as you keep striving to get better, you are never at home, every mistake you make is criticised on social media and the schedule is endless. There are shades of truth in both.

How you feel about these demands will fluctuate, just as your thinking about everything else does. Your perceptions about the demands on you to perform at the level that you play at, always begin as thoughts. These thoughts can become internal stories about whether what you are doing is positive or negative, without you even realising it. These can then form a belief, e.g. "dealing with the media is boring and a waste of my time." You then live within the limitations of that, potentially unhelpful, belief. To reduce stress, understand that the source of stress is within you and not outside of you.

Your capacity to deal with any type of demand on you, on or off the pitch, increases with the knowledge that:

- Everything external is neutral (it is what it is)

- Your thoughts and feelings about the demand will inevitably fluctuate

- You do not have to believe that your current perspective is the only way of seeing it

- If it needs doing, do it

Your game is only one part of your life. If it starts to consume you, and appears to be all that matters in life, you have taken a wrong turn. The path back begins with the recognition that you are not 'John or Jane the Athlete'. Being an athlete or performer in any field is something that you do, not who you are.

It is as important to embrace life outside the game as it is to embrace playing the game itself. Explore what makes you curious and engages you.

You can get so consumed by the game, that you overlook that time away from it can sometimes be the most beneficial thing for performance. Take the time for recovery and to re-energise. Sometimes less is more. Find time to reflect and look at different things, or the same thing from a different angle. You are probably not going to go too far wrong if you spend time on anything that brings a greater appreciation of the natural world, connects you to the people that care about you, allows you to be active or educates you to consider the world in a different light.

Do your interests outside of the game enhance, or detract from, your performance in the game? Why?

The game is great, but there is more to life than the game and more to you as a person than playing it. Just as results on the field cannot directly provide lasting happiness nor cause unhappiness, life away from the game is the same. You do not need 'this' game, 'that' relationship or 'this' social life to be happy. With that knowledge, there is not a necessity for your life to line up exactly as you thought it should. This then, immediately, leaves you freer to navigate it. Understanding this enables you to play full-out and enjoy it, then to walk away at the end of the day, learn from it and move on from it.

Inevitably, your results within the game will determine how long you keep playing. However, it is far less stressful to achieve positive outcomes when you do not believe that the quality of your results determines the quality of your life.

You can slip into a 'rut', and fall into a comfort zone, that prevents you from realising your potential. Your behaviours can become a repetition of what you have done in the past - not because they help, but because doing so is easier than changing.

For you to progress, there will always be external things that you need to move on from. However, it is worth considering that a continual reshuffling of your external environment (places, people, activities) might only give you the same outcomes at a different time and place. If you want a fundamentally different experience externally then you need a different understanding internally.

The support of key people can help you to make sense of what you are doing now and provide guidance on how to progress. These people that you trust, and who will listen, provide both the space for you to clarify your thinking and help if you need it. However, as life continually changes, it is your own understanding of yourself and your perspective on the world that is most important.

What advice would an older, wiser version of yourself give to you right now?

A shift in perspective often appears after big life events. A jolt from the blue disturbs habitual patterns of thinking, and your view on the world changes. However, not everyone has the same changes in perspective after similar life events. By the same token, you do not need a seismic event to occur for you to see things differently. There is always another way to look at, and feel about, the situation that you are in. It is enough just to know that the possibility always exists.

Through understanding your patterns of thinking, your perspective automatically shifts. Old beliefs and ways of behaving no longer make sense, given what you now understand. You do not have to consciously think about how to find perspective or 'headspace'. Despite the best of intentions, the effort to get perspective serves to pile thinking upon thinking which only makes it harder to 'see the wood from the trees'.

As you understand yourself with greater clarity, your priorities will stand out more clearly. Instead of trying to please others or live up to their expectations, your greater sense of perspective allows you to instinctively see what is right, for you.

Are you clear on what matters most to you?

What has been holding you back?

THE OPPONENT

"I judge you unfortunate because you have never lived through misfortune. You have passed through life without an opponent - no one can ever know what you are capable of, not even you."

Seneca

The most important thing to know about your opponent is that *you need them.*

What is the game without an opponent?

More importantly, where is your growth going to come from without an opponent to expose your limitations?

Your opponent's strengths will challenge your weaknesses. Their weaknesses provide opportunities for your strengths.

Of course, you want to win. In the heat of the game, that it is what you are always working towards. However, in considering the bigger picture of realising your potential, there is not an opponent in the world who does not provide the chance for you to surpass your previous results and your perceived limitations. A team or player that is far better than you will teach you what it takes to be better and, if needed, how to lose with grace. A team or player that is not as good as you teaches you how to be clinical and how to win with humility.

Although everybody wants to win, what you are really

looking for is an opponent who takes you to the edge of your abilities. Most of the time it is far more rewarding to lose having given everything possible, than having won with plenty still left in the tank. It is those hard-fought, intense matches, series or competitions that can create a sense of togetherness between opponents, even though it might often be a non-verbal acknowledgment and understanding of each other. It comes from the knowledge that you have both given everything that you could and that you shook the edges of each other's game until the result fell one way or another by the smallest margin.

Competition can bring out the best in you when you understand how essential your opponent is to you. However, if you believe that they are not there *for* you but, instead, are playing *against* you then it increases the feeling of insecurity which can bring out the worst in you. The belief that competition is 'you against the world' immediately divides the game into winners and losers, with you trying to be a winner. You start with beating one opponent then another and then another. At every level, the ratio of losers to winners increases, until there is only one winner - a champion. It ends up with only one winner and roughly eight billion losers.

This division of the game into winners and losers is created when you believe that you *need* to win. You believe that you need to be better than others so that you can be validated, 'be somebody', to be able to enjoy yourself or even just to be OK. In which case, you are looking for winning to give you something that it cannot provide.

Winning is enjoyable and it should be pursued and appreciated when it happens. However, it is not the answer to some of the bigger questions you might (knowingly or unknowingly) hope that it could be. Results will always create winners and losers on the surface but, underneath that, what you get out of it depends on the understanding that you have on what competition is for.

For the ego, which is intent on proving itself, the 'us against the world' mentality can provide an edge that helps an individual to 'get up' for a 'battle'. However, when you play *against* your opponent rather than *with* them, you play in fear. In fear that if you lose the game, you lose your validation. You end up hoping that the opposition's best player is injured, or that the conditions will be stacked in your favour. These are insecure thoughts that, if believed, force you to perform *under* pressure. The belief that you *need* to win traps you and restricts you from going beyond these perceptions.

The game's challenges are fundamental, not only to winning but also to the deeper process of self-discovery. Learn what your opponent is capable of - their strengths and weaknesses, their method and how they adapt - so that you can meet the challenge of facing them. The more challenging the obstacles that you encounter, the greater the opportunity that they provide for you to uncover your true potential.

When you are competing *with* your opponent, you are absorbed in the exploration of the yet unknown depths of your capabilities. Even if, at times, it feels like you are playing *against* your opponent it still helps to know that, on a deeper level, you are competing *with* them. This gives you a greater sense of perspective. It is great to win, but you do not need to be 'a winner'. Winning is a temporary outcome in the game, it is not who you are.

The bigger questions about winning and happiness can only be answered by your own self-knowledge. By understanding who you are, with or without the game, you can play the game as if it means everything while knowing that it does not. It allows you to compete full-out in competition with your opponent as their rising standard forces your abilities upwards and vice-versa. Your opponent is the best teammate, coach and mentor that you will ever get, and they will probably never know it.

There will be opponents that push you to the edge in ways beyond your skills and abilities. It is almost as if they can get 'under your skin', 'push your buttons' and leave you focused more on them than the game itself.

During the game, your opponents' behaviour might feel distracting. This can be behaviour directed towards you (e.g. 'sledging') or indirectly (e.g. feigning injuries). You will get caught up in these behaviours for as long as you believe that they are relevant. Some players thrive on 'trash talk'. Others find it to be a battle of egos that does not make them any better or induces them into making mistakes. This can happen when they try to prove a point instead of playing each ball as it comes.

When opponents *appear* to make you feel this way, it might not be enough just to know that your opponent is there *for* you. They are exposing the fault lines in your perceptions and it is easy to want a quick fix for that. However, quick fixes prescribed by someone else (as opposed to your own insight about how to handle the situation) are usually ineffective. Even if they work for the moment, by papering over the cracks (perhaps with a mental technique), your understanding has not deepened in any way. The effect of the 'fix' will wear off, and you will end up searching for your next quick fix.

In and of itself, there is nothing wrong with getting angry at an opponent or frustrated with a match situation. Problems arise with the idea that you should not be angry. With this belief, you are likely to try to control your inner experience or change the situation that appears to be determining how you feel (an 'outside-in' illusion). However, if you feel angry, it is fine. Allow yourself to feel that way.

In accepting anger when it occurs, it neither lasts nor

impacts you for as long as the normal habit of resisting it would. It is absolutely OK to feel the way that you feel at any moment. It is far more effective in the long run to understand how your experience works from within, and be OK with it all, than it is to believe that certain elements of it are more 'right' than others.

The root of someone else's words begins with an inherently, illusory thought which makes enough sense to them to verbalise. It does not help to believe your own thinking, let alone getting wrapped up in that of someone else. Although they are unlikely to put it into these words, when a player 'sledges' they are attempting to attack your sense of self. If their words are taken personally, your feelings of self-consciousness can increase to the point that you are no longer playing the game instinctively. This is why knowing yourself makes all the difference, because there becomes no rigid sense of identity for them to attack.

You are going to face skilful opponents with big reputations. You can get caught up with who you are facing and lose focus on what you are doing. However, everyone (including the very best) is subject to the fluctuations of their inner experience in addition to the peaks and troughs of their performances and results.

Great performers get insecure, nervous and anxious too. They might be good at hiding it, or too technically and tactically superior for their opponent. Or they might understand their inner experience with the clarity that experiencing these thoughts and feelings does not inhibit them. However, they experience these fluctuations all the same. They have days when their game is out of sync and they cannot find their rhythm. They have bad days. They experience conditions which are not as suited to them or situations to which they find it hard to adapt.

Without seeing others as they truly are, you can end up putting certain teams or players on a pedestal in your mind. You can believe that they are 'so good', almost 'super-human', that you miss the opportunities to put their game to the test. No matter how good someone is, what their past achievements have been or how intimidating their persona might seem, they are not unbeatable. There are flaws in everybody's game – a key part of the game is finding them.

When you get caught up in 'playing the man and not the ball', the key lies in simplicity. Play the game as it comes and do the best you can from where you are. After a match, you can take the opportunity to see more clearly what you were getting caught up in and learn from it. Reflect on the thoughts that looked so important and compelling at the time, to see them for what they were. In the midst of the game, 'playing *this* ball' is not always going to feel easy. However, with an ever-deepening perspective on yourself, the game and your opponent, the answers begin to occur intuitively.

OBSTACLES BEYOND THE OPPONENT

"Your external environment simply reflects your internal environment. Your internal environment simply reflects your beliefs, and only you hold the key to them."

James Blanchard Cisneros

At times, it can feel like your biggest obstacle is not the opponent standing opposite you, but something else on the periphery. This might be the score on the board, the crowd or the occasion. When people say that they were distracted by these factors, it is never actually those things directly impacting them. They get caught in their thinking *about* them. Without realising, they then try to think their way out of the situation. This only takes them further away from their natural capacity to perform.

The score becomes an obstacle when the way that you play is dependent entirely on it, rather than responding to the match situation as it develops. The scoreboard is informative but you cannot play the scoreboard, you just have to play the ball in front of you.

A classic example is a cricket batsman on 99 runs who tenses up and finds it impossible to score the final run for their century, despite scoring freely moments before. If you did not know the perceived importance of scoring a century in cricket, you would not play any differently. However, with the belief that this run matters more than the others, you intellectually try to work your way forward, rather than trusting in yourself to keep playing the game.

The audience at a match seem to have a big impact on performance. A home crowd can feel so empowering; their energy can make it feel like you have an extra player on your team. However, their hope, expectation and desire for you to win can also feel like a burden. An opposing audience can be intimidating with so many people cheering against you, hoping that you lose. However, playing in front of an opposing audience can also be invigorating when you silence the noise and earn their respect with your performance. A large crowd can be exciting. A large crowd can be daunting. A small crowd, or an empty stadium, can feel lifeless. A small, or no, crowd can seem freeing as there is no-one there to judge you.

There is only one true conclusion; the crowd as a factor is inherently neutral. If you think that a home or an opposing crowd, a large or a small audience, is a big deal then that is how it will feel. This is because thought and feeling are joined at the seams and not because crowds can influence how you play (even when it feels like they can).

As thoughts and feelings fluctuate, your perceptions about whether a type of crowd is a good or a bad thing will ebb and flow too. While your inner experience and interpretations will change, your capacity to adapt and play in the moment is always there.

When you become 'successful', other people will have their views on it. Trying to match the expectations of other people can make it feel like they are putting pressure on you. Most of the time, people with high expectations of you (e.g. coaches and family) only want the best for you. When people with genuinely good intentions appear to be putting pressure on you, take a step back. See how the way that they communicate these good intentions has started to get muddled. Often, they want you to be happy and they think that by you achieving a certain outcome, then you will be. Therefore, they believe that by you achieving it and being happy, then they will be happy too. This is all backwards - it is outside-in thinking.

By being able to see an almost innocence in the way that those people are thinking, and therefore communicating, you will have a sense of clarity to talk to them, to reassess the relationship if needed and to explain how they can best support you. Other people, even with the best of intentions, get caught up in their own thinking and projections too.

If others' high expectations, best wishes or opinions begin to feel like a burden, consider:

Why do you feel that you should live up to someone else's expectations?
Who are you trying to impress and why?
Does it help or hinder you by doing so?

You do not need to, nor is it even possible to, keep other people happy through your performances. It is nice to feel appreciated, valued and even celebrated. However, it is not needed. What is needed far more is for you to be yourself - your natural, authentic self - to do your best and to know that you are OK no matter what happens or what anyone else thinks of you.

Dealing with judgment or criticism is not about having to be strong or weak, it is about being open enough to allow it all to pass through. You do not have to hold on to, or analyse, someone else's perspective once they have said it. Even saying "everyone is entitled to their opinion" is making something out of it where it is not necessary. When you understand that these views are all transient, illusory thoughts, they will naturally flow straight through unless there is an interesting lesson to learn. If you do not energise them, those thoughts have no life.

If someone feels that the best way for them to feel good about themselves is to belittle others, it is because they are feeling insecure themselves. They are trying to give their ego a boost. This will happen from time-to-time because everyone feels insecure at times. Those people that are more attached to their sense of identity - their ego - will behave in this way more frequently. It happens less as a person becomes more comfortable in themself.

Comparison is an incredibly useful way of making sense of the world. Comparison provides information about where you are at and tells you what you need to learn. However, if you end up comparing yourself to others, because you feel that by being better than them, then you will feel better you have taken a wrong turn.

You are surrounded by people who are like you in many

ways and different in as many others. You are going to notice what they are doing and the results this creates. It is often said that "comparison is the thief of joy". However, it only becomes unhealthy when observation turns into judgment. It does not matter if you are judging yourself or another person, you are the one who ends up experiencing the negativity that these judgments create.

Any comparison with others involves creating an image of yourself in your mind - who you think you are and how you think that you are doing - and an image of the other person. Both these images are thoughts. Thoughts should be taken for what they are. There is no value in creating negativity in your own mind, through turning an initial comparative thought into something that you use to judge yourself or others.

The only value in comparison is to learn. If you use comparison to influence your sense of self - temporarily making you feel better through an 'ego boost' - it only takes you further away from who you are. No two journeys are alike. You have to discover what you need to learn.

PBP KEY #2 UNDERSTAND THE GAME: SUMMARY

1. The game *is* a game. A game to be played, enjoyed and to be figured out. To win and to lose at. The circumstances may change, but at the heart of it, it is still the same game as it ever was.

2. Recall the natural and intuitive enjoyment of the game that you had when you started playing.

3. Rewards should be a by-product of doing what you love. However, if they become your primary motivation then they drain the enjoyment out of the game.

4. There are no inherent 'big moments', they are a perception based on the meaning that you place on the outcome of the game.

5. Practice and competition can merge into each other. Play the game as it comes, rather than putting certain matches, people or places on artificial, mind-made

pedestals.

6. Embrace what you need to do to perform at your best. Prioritise, balance and let go of what needs to be, externally and internally. Remember that your feelings about all the game's demands are always going to fluctuate.

7. Performing is what you do, it is not who you are.

8. Opponents are the benchmarks that allow you to know where you are at and what you need to improve. The better your opponent, the better you can become.

9. You will get riled by opponents when you are deriving your sense of self from the game. As your attachment to your identity loosens, it becomes more straightforward to 'play the ball and not the man'.

10. Everything external to you (e.g. opponent, crowd, venue, conditions and the match situation) is inherently neutral. Your capacity to see things as they are is what enables you to progress without the stress.

KEY #3 PLAY YOUR GAME

- **Trust Your Instincts**

- **Concentration**

- **Be Comfortable Feeling Uncomfortable**

- **Your Adapted Method**

- **Mastery**

- **Success and Failure**

TRUST YOUR INSTINCTS

"No matter how hard a surfer works, the ocean is doing most of the heavy lifting."

Consider that an 'instinctive presence' might be your fundamental nature. For the time being, assume that beliefs, perceptions, thoughts, and feelings form an illusory layer that lie on top of your fundamental nature. These layers that hold you back will be removed automatically as you see yourself, and the game, with a deeper understanding.

Instincts are your unconscious intelligence. Consider the full scale and power of unconscious intelligence. It rotates planets on their axis, turns plants towards the sun and regenerates the cells of your body. Instinct is how you learnt to walk without any idea of how or why. Having developed your sporting abilities, instinct enables you to perform your skills without really having to think about it. This is why many top sportspeople achieve amazing feats without always being able to describe it or analyse how.

With faith in your instincts, you become attuned to what is taking place in the moment. When you are more present - and therefore not distracted by any thought, feeling or external factor - you play each ball, on its merits, as it comes. You can perform to your potential, even when you do not feel that it is possible.

When you feel under pressure you are experiencing insecure thoughts and perceptions. Your ability to perform is as hindered, or helped, by these feelings as much as you believe it to be. The way that you feel does not have any power to stop you doing what you are capable of, despite how it can appear. You are always able to perform because there is an intelligence within you that is more powerful than temporary perceptions: Instinct.

Intellect is a form of intelligence that develops as you grow older. It is the conscious intelligence allowing you to compare, judge, memorise and explain. The intellect is great for formulating game plans, assessing the match situation and reflecting on your performances to learn. It allows you to understand the complexity of the game and adapt your strategy.

When you feel insecure or the game is not going to plan, there is a temptation to use the intellect to think your way out of it. However, if you try to consciously think about every movement required, you can turn even the simplest of physical actions into something that feels unnatural and it becomes ineffective. However, this is what we sometimes do to ourselves when feeling anxious on the sports field.

When the time comes to physically move, the deeper instinctive intelligence should be free to 'just do it'. If you instead try to control your performance with the intellect by deliberately thinking about how, where and when to move or strike, you only end up getting in your own way. You end up 'choking'. 'Choking' is when the intellect hijacks your instincts, and previously habitual movements become tense and erratic. When a performer attempts to control a route to success with conscious thinking rather than naturally playing the game, it is often said that the person is 'trying too hard'.

When you make an error in a match, there is a temptation to try to consciously correct it. If you sent the ball more to the right than you wanted, you might think about trying to send it more to the left next time. However, you are likely to end up over-correcting and sending the ball too far the other way. Then you try to correct yourself again but might end up dragging it short and so on, until you are completely lost and are just looking for any way out.

To overcome 'choking' and the 'yips', go back to the root cause.
What do you believe about yourself and your results that causes you to tense up?

When you make a mistake on the field, know that it is just a mistake. Be aware of it, but you do not need to read anything more into it. Noticing it is enough. By noticing it you know what has happened and so natural learning can take place. You do not need to be down on yourself for having made the error or to try to 'make up for it'.

Rather than focusing on what is a happening in the match, it can become a habit to drag what happened with the last ball or in the last game into the current one. Or to worry about what you think will, or might, happen. These concerns about what you want (e.g. lifting the trophy, the celebrations) or what you are seeking to avoid (e.g. getting dropped, being criticised), can lead to rushing or a sense of frustration. Holding onto these ideas creates an intellectual process that only gets in the way of your natural, instinctive best.

During a match, the analytical thinking about the 'how and why' of a mistake only makes it more likely that another mistake will happen. This is because your attention is on the past and not what is happening in the present. As you realise that fixating on mistakes provides no value once you have learned from them, the habit of obsessing over them falls away. Without further energising them, thoughts - 'positive' and 'negative' - flow through and your attention is back where it needs to be.

You cannot *try* to be 'present' or instinctive. This trying involves additional, intellectual thinking which puts your attention on the trying and not on what is happening. Trying to be instinctive is the opposite of being instinctive. You just end up thinking about your thinking rather than just playing the game in front of you. Your intellect wants to control the situation but, instead, let go and allow your instincts to take over.

It is amazing how often the ball will go where it needs to when you do not mind where it ends up. Naturally, you want to perform well, but it is more valuable to approach a contest with a sense of exploration rather than expectation. Let go of control and trust your instincts to play the game - in the same way that you do with normal physical activities, such as walking down the street or driving your car. The reason that you rarely hijack these 'normal' activities with your intellect is that you have not created such a sense of meaning about them.

People are more instinctive - and therefore able to adapt to what is required in the moment - when they have faith in their instincts. Instinct is not controllable or measurable. It requires knowing that your full potential lies beyond conscious, intellectual thinking. This understanding frees you up to respond to what is needed in the moment, unburdened by what you *think* that you know or how you wish the situation to be. You can react to reality as you find it.

You will not always feel certainty. Having faith in your instincts means that you are also OK with not knowing exactly what to do. You take the action that makes sense in the moment. You are not paralysed by a need for everything to be in order and in the right place. You know that, if you need to, you can work it out as you go and play it as it comes. As you naturally and instinctively play the game, your performance can surpass all your own expectations. You might play in a way that makes you think "I didn't realise I was *that* good!"

When you trust your 'gut', you begin to intuitively anticipate the game. It might appear from the outside that you are 'one step ahead', almost as if you knew what was going to happen. When *letting go* and allowing it to *flow* becomes a natural habit, you read the game and act instinctively even before your conscious thinking has had time to catch up. This prevents overthinking the situation or even *trying* to think about it. You feel absorbed, connected and quietly present. The game comes to you, rather than you trying to force it.

People sometimes describe these experiences of high performance as almost 'out of body' experiences. What they have felt is the experience of 'losing themselves'. Everyone has had that feeling at some point, whether it is on the sports field, listening to music or watching a movie. It might appear in other parts of your life where your sense of identity is not so reliant on the outcome, and without the belief that *this* performance is more important than *that* one. By not getting caught up in expectations or judgments, there is no self-image to protect or prove and so instinct is free to take over.

Trusting your instincts means letting your body strike, throw or bowl the ball. Do not try to be instinctive. Know that this is possible and allow it to happen. You have to experience this for yourself, rather than through intellectual analysis. Play with fun, with freedom and without inhibitions. You have done all the practice, now trusting your instincts is about trusting yourself.

CONCENTRATION

"If you are interested in something, you will focus on it. Flow is being completely involved in an activity for its own sake. The ego falls away. Time flies. Every action, movement, and thought follows inevitably from the previous one, like playing jazz."

Mihaly Csikszentmihalyi

When instinct takes over, you are concentrating. Concentration is only broken by being distracted by your own thinking. It is not the opponent, the crowd or the scoreboard that disturbs concentration, it is your thinking *about* them.

Concentration is straightforward when you are doing what you love. It is so much simpler than trying to 'focus' or 'switch on'. It is not effortful, it is inevitable. You are absorbed, but it is not a strain.

Why would you have to try hard to concentrate at doing something that you love?

The more that you are trying to 'get' something (e.g. a contract, selection, validation from others), over and above playing your best in the moment, the more that you have to *try* to concentrate. This is because you will experience a lot of thinking about where you are trying to get to or what you think will happen if you do not succeed. You will feel that you must effortfully eliminate those thoughts to be able to focus back in on the match. However, this becomes a vicious circle because it is not possible to control thinking with more thinking.

You cannot effortfully concentrate and you do *not* need to try. You only end up adding more thinking, rather than just playing. Concentration is a term that can only be applied looking backwards. When you just keep playing and keep enjoying yourself, you might reflect on the game and think "Wow, I was really in 'the zone' and did not even realise it!"

Your attention will inevitably waver at times. However, do not blame that on 'distractions'. There are always a lot of external factors going on for everyone in every circumstance. However, the degree to which any of them appear to 'distract' you only depends on the amount of time that you spend thinking about them. Despite how another person or a task can *feel* like a distraction, at another time or in another place you would not be distracted by them or it in the same way. Therefore, avoid believing that something outside of you determines how engaged you are. You can only be distracted by your own thoughts.

'Switching on and off' should be an intuitive process,

rather than a conscious one. As old patterns of thinking, that used to consume you fall by the wayside, intuition naturally regulates your attention based on what you are dealing with and what is required. If you find yourself regularly losing concentration - i.e. you are no longer absorbed in the game - reflect on what is getting in the way of something that is natural and instinctive.

What is the internal story that is distracting from the simple, immersion in playing the game?

How has your perspective on the game changed so that you now feel that you need to effortfully attempt to concentrate?

Concentration is a term that describes what happens when you are instinctively playing the game. It is a natural state of being. If you do not feel focused, attempting to control your attention or to attribute your state of mind to an external 'distraction' only takes you further away from being immersed in what you are doing. Trying to concentrate is a quick fix, but you must look beyond that to find a transformative answer to being fully engaged in the game. Consider what perception or belief is preventing this natural process of concentrating from taking place.

This is a reminder to simplify your approach. To play with full-out commitment with the sheer enjoyment of the game at the forefront. The more that you trust your instincts and love what you are doing, the more your experience of playing will naturally feel like effortless 'concentration'. As you play with this inner understanding, it will no longer make sense to give up on a game until the final whistle goes. You play every ball as if it is your first and your last.

BE COMFORTABLE FEELING UNCOMFORTABLE

"I have self-doubt. I have insecurity. I have fear of failure. I have nights when I show up at the arena and I'm like, 'My back hurts, my feet hurt, my knees hurt. I don't have it. I just want to chill.' We all have self-doubt. You don't deny it, but you also don't capitulate to it. You embrace it."

Kobe Bryant

To perform beyond pressure, you have to embrace both difficulty and discomfort. The way that you feel will always change, but your ability and capacity to play your game are what remains the same. Being comfortable feeling uncomfortable enables you to navigate the game when either your inner state or the outer situation is challenging.

This happens when you know that:

- You can perform however you are feeling (i.e. trust your instincts)

- You are OK no matter what happens

You perform however you are feeling when you understand that, while your inner experience is always in a state of flux, your instincts and ability level are far more stable. You *can* play great even if it feels like you might not be able to.

When you understand that your internal experience is in a perpetual state of ebb and flow, then you embrace that. Not just the parts that make you feel good, but in its totality. You realise that an element of discomfort is essential for growth. You cannot stretch your limits if you are feeling comfortable all the time.

Instinct is always there despite the changes in psychological weather that you experience. As you see this for yourself, you realise that you do not have to feel good in order to play great. Everyone has felt so nervous that it *feels like* they are going to perform badly but, once they get into the game, instinct takes over and they end up playing brilliantly. Of course, by the same token, the opposite is always possible too - you might feel 'on top of the world' and then make a mistake or not play your best.

This shows that there is no value in reading much into the way that you feel immediately before a match. If you feel calm and relaxed, great. If you feel nervous and anxious, great. You are still the same player, you can still play the game, just get out onto the field and get going with faith in your instincts.

It can be assumed that 'the zone' is such a blissful experience that if you are 'in it', everything will work out and all your problems will be solved. While it can seem like that, this is only in retrospect. Performance ebbs and flows, just as your internal experience does. Great performances can feel like a struggle at times. Therefore, searching for a certain state of mind such as 'the zone' is a red herring. This search only takes you further away from your natural capacity to adapt and realise your potential.

Even when you are feeling deeply uncomfortable (e.g. anxious or nervous), your capacity to instinctively perform has not gone anywhere. Leave insecure thoughts to come and go. Your moods and emotions are transient. It is inevitable that the way that you feel now is going to be different to how you feel in an hour's time. If you are nervous now, you will not be nervous forever. Even the most ingrained patterns of thinking shift of their own accord through the course of a day.

Feeling uncomfortable and uncertain is OK. Playing in the wide-open space of *not knowing* what will happen is far more rewarding and freeing, than being confined by the 'play-it-safe' limitations that look compelling when you want to feel differently. You may also realise that the idea of feeling great all the time is not the elixir that you might have imagined it to be. You will find out far more about yourself by going through the fire as well as the ice, the darkness and the light - the whole rollercoaster.

There is an obsession with confidence. Confidence is the feeling that arises in the absence of doubtful, anxious and insecure thinking. Without that thinking clouding your perspective, you would feel comfortable with the situation. This is why children are often far more confident than adults. It is not how good you are that provides confidence, it is the lack of identifying with thoughts that detract from your natural well-being and confidence.

Confidence is a feeling that people who are always looking to the past, or the future, try desperately to hold on to. However, the more you believe that you need confidence to perform then the less confident you will become. It is the contingencies that you place on confidence that gets in the way of experiencing it, e.g. "I need confidence" or "If X happens then I will feel confident." Nobody is going to feel confident all the time, no matter how good they are or what their social media posts attempt to portray.

Avoid trying to cling on to confidence, it will just make you anxious. Allow confidence to come and go and you will come to a deeper sense of 'OK-ness' however you are feeling and whatever you are doing.

The absence of feeling confident creates the illusion that you are not capable. However, see the illusion for what it is. You have not changed; you are still the same player. Let go of the belief that you hold about what you think needs to happen in the game for you to be able to feel confident. Let go of the belief about what you think that the feeling of confidence will give you, that you do not have already.

Become aware of your beliefs about confidence.

Are you sure that they are true, or can you find any example when they were not?

When you know that you do not have to feel confident - that it is meant to come and go - then learning how to play your best in the face of insecure thinking ('being comfortable feeling uncomfortable') becomes far more straightforward. You see those thoughts and feelings as nothing more than the transient perceptions that they are, rather than as a determinant of how well you will perform. Without the attention on whether you are confident or not, you get on with immersing yourself in the game. When you are absorbed in playing the game, you do not have the time or interest to be too concerned about it. You just keep going with the ebb and the flow of the game. Then confidence returns to its natural rise and fall, just as all other thoughts and feelings do.

Knowing that you are OK no matter what happens is the realisation that what happens does not define you. Your worth and happiness do not come from the results you achieve. Who you are lies far beyond the good days and the bad days, triumphs and failures, pleasure and pain. Who you are lies at the root of everything that you experience. It is normal to prefer wins to losses, but it is natural to be OK with both.

For many performers, their sense of self-worth is tied up in the results that they achieve. This stems from cultural conditioning that tells us that the *better* we are then the more *important* we are and so, the better we will *feel*. This conditioning gets it backwards and creates a pressure to perform where it need not exist. If you end up believing this cultural conditioning to be true, then every time that you go out on to the field you are under pressure to prove yourself, not only as an athlete but also as a human being.

The better that you get, the more tempting it can be to take the game seriously and believe that results determine who you are. If your livelihood depends on the results, the game can quickly stop feeling like a game at all. You stop playing and start 'having to perform'. While there is a logic to this, it only serves to get in the way of realising your potential.

Know who you are, with or without your results. For as long as you feel that you are 'a failure' or 'a winner', you are neither. Everything in the game, and everything outside of it, will change - that is the nature of life. Express yourself freely with that knowledge. When you know yourself, you know that you really are OK however the game plays out.

YOUR ADAPTED METHOD

"No man ever steps in the same river twice, for it's not the same river and he's not the same man."

Heraclitus

To succeed at the game, you need to be skilled and have the tactical knowledge of when and how to apply that ability. Your adapted method is your own natural, best way of playing combined with an understanding of the game. The knowledge of *your* game within *the* game enables you to adjust to the challenges of each match situation.

There is no one way to succeed. There are often key fundamentals that are required to achieve success in every sport. However, for as much as top players may have in common, there are always notable differences in their main strengths (e.g. power vs. guile, attack vs. defence, structure vs. creativity etc.). Your method is your way of playing. Your individual combination of technique, options, tempo and rhythm. Your method develops as you learn more about the game and what delivers success for you.

What are the fundamentals of your game that are unlikely to change, regardless of the circumstances?

How will you need to develop your abilities to play at higher levels?

How can you play when your skills are being stretched and tested?

There is no technique or strategy that is guaranteed to work for you, no matter how well it worked for someone else. The way that you move and play the game is a unique combination of your genetics and the experiences that you have had within the game from a formative age. Understand why you move and play the way that you do and what it is that makes you successful.

Pursue substance over style - find out what works for you. Maximise what you have and who you are. Follow your instincts about how to play the game in a way that feels natural to you. When you find the approach that helps you to perform at your best most often, your individuality will naturally emerge. Then you will understand your natural style and your natural best, and so will not second guess yourself.

How do you play when everything is smooth, rhythmical and feels natural?

Everyone has a blend of strengths and limitations. There

is a difference between talents, strengths and a learned skill. Talents are primarily genetically predisposed. Some people are naturally more athletic, coordinated or balanced than others. However, on its own, talent does not lead to lasting success.

When a talent is repeatedly worked on, it becomes a strength. Be clear on what your strengths are and trust them in the game. If you only do one or two things well, the opposition can more easily cut off those options. The more breadth and depth of skill that your game has, the more readily you will adjust to the variety of challenges that you face. When you turn some of your strengths into 'super-strengths' it provides you with a clear approach to being successful.

Understand and make peace with your weaknesses. You are not going to be, nor need to be, perfect. By acknowledging your weaknesses as they are and being OK with having them, you can develop strategies that work around the areas of your game that are not as strong. This will equip you to prevent opponents from exposing them while not losing the capacity to capitalise on your strengths. In practice, look to improve the areas of your game that do not come so naturally. These can turn into 'learned skills'. While proficiency might not come as naturally as it does for your talents, 'learned skills' can become highly effective components of your method.

Keep your method as simple as you can. As you get better there are more variables at play, and so it becomes easy to complicate things. The more that you learn, the easier it is to overlook your natural strengths. Have clarity on what you do and how you do it best so that, in the heat of the moment, your instincts can take over.

You are not going to be as good at some skills as the person next to you, but they are also not as good as you at other things. You must play the hand that you have been dealt. Work out what makes you, "You", and focus on making your skillset the most effective that it can be.

There is a critical distinction to be made between being aware of the limits of your game and the limits created in your mind. Knowing your strengths and playing to them, means that you understand ways of playing that are high reward and lower risk. Psychological limitations are those that prevent you from playing to those strengths or from learning from the experience.

On their own, thoughts such as "I am not good enough" and "I am never going to get better" are harmless and illusory. However, if they are identified with and believed, they become psychological limitations. As with all beliefs, they shape your experience, and you will search for evidence that appears to prove that belief to be true.

These initial thoughts can become a self-fulfilling prophecy. The more that you believe that you are not good enough, the more evidence you will find to back that up and, in doing so, the more your results will reflect it. This cycle is broken with the recognition of the nature of those original thoughts. You notice how easy it can be to erroneously believe what you think. With that realisation, your focus automatically shifts back towards the endless potential outcomes. This insight means that optimism and anticipation naturally replace self-pity and frustration.

It is one thing to understand the inherent strengths and limitations of your game as it stands right now. However, it is another to know how and when to utilise them given the opponent, the conditions and the match situation.

You are always able to adapt. You become more skilled at it when you understand:

- That you are naturally adaptable

- The tactics available to play the match situation

"It is not the most intellectual of the species that survives; it is not the strongest that survives; but the species that survives is the one that is able best to adapt and adjust to the changing environment in which it finds itself."
- Charles Darwin

Adaptability is a part of your nature. You are always evolving and so is the game. Adapting is reading the situation, utilising different skills, and playing different roles based on what is required of you right now.

Your capacity to perform can be hindered by ideas that pen you in to believing that there is only one way of doing it, or by 'paralysis by analysis' where you get 'caught in thought'. Through overthinking the situation, you lose faith in your instincts and the importance of playing one ball at a time.

Every game poses different scenarios and challenges. You can only adapt if you understand the ways in which the match, in that moment, is challenging you. Adapting is identifying what the situation is asking of you, what you can do about it and then doing it.

The longer that you have been playing the game, the more times you will have previously faced situations that require you to adapt. This enables you to learn from experience. However, there are times when you can still make the same mistakes over and over. This is because you have become locked into the same habitual patterns of thinking about the game. This prevents you from considering deeply enough whether there might be another way.

View each situation exactly as it is. Neither inherently good nor bad, but simply the opportunity and the challenge that lies immediately in front of you. What has gone before is no longer relevant once you have learnt from it. Neither is contemplating what you think that the consequences of the result might be.

Seeing the situation as it is means accepting it completely even if it is far, far different from the scenario that you were hoping for. You might be disappointed, frustrated or upset when you encounter circumstances that differ from expectations. However, do not get caught up in an internal story about why the conditions or circumstances are a problem, and 'throw in the towel' before you have started.

If the situation is, in theory, more in favour of your opponent then there is no need to hide away from that. It is what it is. The more you argue with the reality of the situation, the more tension and frustration you will experience. While situations that are not in your favour can initially seem like a problem, they are in fact an opportunity. To realise your potential, you will have to find a way to succeed when it is difficult even more often than when it appears to be easier. It is through acceptance, and understanding, of what you are facing that you will see what can be done and how.

The conditions in which you play are always changing. From home and away, the size and speed of the playing surface, to the weather. Consider the F.A. Cup in football - you could be playing in front of small crowd on a muddy pitch in one round and then in front of a crowd of 60,000 on a large, pristine surface, in the next. Or in tennis, where players come straight off the clay courts into the grass court season. As well as varying conditions, there will be the wide range of match situations that you will face - e.g. in cricket being 10 for 3 in a Test match or 80 for 0 in T20 cricket. The more that you understand what each situation is asking of you, the more seamlessly you will adapt. Every match, and every situation within the match, is a test.

There is an ebb and flow to any contest, just as there is with your inner experience while playing it. There will be tactical needs to shift up and down 'the gears', adapting your game to the ever-changing dynamic of the match. You may be on top in the game, but then have to readjust to the situation or opponent. The balance of restricting your opponent and imposing your strengths will keep shifting. The risk and reward of the options that you have are never the same from one moment to the next as the match situation, the conditions and your opponent's way of playing alter.

The hardest opponents to play against are those who can read the game and play as best fits the need in that situation - they can play fast or slow, be physical or skillful, play when ahead on the scoreboard or behind. Sometimes it pays to focus purely on what you can do and take the necessary risks that might go with that. At other times you will have to learn to play 'in your shadow', e.g. a naturally attacking player capable of defensive high performance. Your method of playing will suit some situations more than others, but effective performers are those that adapt to play the role that is required of them on the day. The game challenges you to keep evolving, adapting and building these skills, while remaining true to your strengths and your natural best way of playing.

What is your best role?
How do you play that role when the contest is going your way, and how do you adjust when it is not?

What other roles do you, or can you, play?

The art of adapting is finding a way. Work out your best options for different match scenarios given your strengths and the external factors creating the specific situation. Once you are clear on your game plan, let go and allow your instincts to take over. Your best performances will come when you begin to intuitively recognise the need to adapt. Then you will perform with the ebb and the flow of the game.

"When you have exhausted all possibilities, remember this: you haven't."
- Thomas Edison

MASTERY

"One can have no smaller or greater mastery than mastery of oneself."

Leonardo Da Vinci

Mastery is the process of realising your potential through the ongoing learning and application of *your* game to *the* game. You never know what your full potential might be. You must find your own path to becoming the best performer that you can be.

Mastery has two components:

- Learning
- Doing 'The Work'

Your capacity to learn is infinite. Everyone may have innate, genetic limitations and natural talents, but that does not mean that there is any limit to your capacity to learn. No matter where you are starting from, you can always learn from this point onwards.

Lots of people want a shortcut to being successful. They think that being successful, and everything that might come with that, will make them happy. However, this search for happiness in the game is precisely what prevents the experience of it. When this is understood, learning is no longer a means to an end (a route to happiness), it becomes the end in itself. Results become lessons as well as outcomes.

Why would you want a shortcut, if you knew that learning was as rewarding as the outcome?

When you give up trying to get the external world to fix how you feel internally - i.e. the desire for results to create happiness - then improvement becomes fun again. You will still experience the ups and downs of your inner experience. However, you will realise how much enjoyment lies purely in the path of discovery.

> *"The journey is the destination."*
> *- Ralph Waldo Emerson*

For most people, learning used to be easier. Now it has become slower and more frustrating. The primary reason for this is because they now filter the world through all their beliefs and perceptions. They no longer see everything with a freshness. They see everything through a lens of how they expect it to be. Therefore, things no longer appear as they actually are.

You might avoid situations that appear to make you feel

uncomfortable. You might find it hard to learn because of the discomfort that comes from replaying bad days, and your mistakes, over and over in your mind. However, these are 'outside-in' illusions. The emotions that you experience at these times stem only from your transient interpretations of what has, or might, happen. However, it is the experiences that are beyond your comfort zone that have the most potential to teach you about yourself and the game.

When you think that you already know what is going to happen, you become closed off to the possibilities of what *could* happen. Another person's advice might be uncomfortable to hear because it threatens your sense of identity. Attachment to that sense of self means that you become more focused on protecting your viewpoint than listening with an open mind. You might try to give the impression that you have everything under control and avoid asking for guidance. Ask yourself whether the information offered is truly not relevant right now because of the path that you are on, or whether it only feels that way because of an unconscious act of self-preservation. Sometimes, the advice you do not want to hear, is the advice you need.

Zen has a term called a 'beginner's mind'. This is the experience of being wide open to whatever might happen. When you embrace uncertainty and 'not knowing' then what happens can far surpass your previous expectations. Mastery creates the knowledge that, no matter how much you know, there is always more to learn. Here, you are free of preconceptions about how anything works or what will happen. You are filled with curiosity to understand things more deeply, and open up to a world of possibilities.

This open mind allows you to keep evolving. When you set targets and limits for what success is, it is easy to be complacent once you have achieved them. This comfort is pleasant, but it does not last. If you do not move forwards as a player, you will go backwards once others figure out your game or you move up to the level. When you are open to learning, you can look ahead to what you need to succeed at the next stage before you get there.

There is wisdom everywhere. It may be from coaches, teachers and mentors, or from teammates and friends, or from a world-class performer or even a novice. People's rate of learning can be hindered because they think there are some people from whom they can learn and some from whom they cannot. Some people have more expertise in your field and therefore the odds of them being able to help are higher. However, lessons can come from the most unexpected of sources. Even if this is just through observing how others do it so that you can figure out all the ways that you will *not*. If you are curious enough to find out then the whole game, and everybody within it, can be your teacher. Every experience provides an opportunity to shape you for the better.

What another person or an event can teach you might not land as a lesson in the moment that it occurs. However, with hindsight it might all make sense, or a similar lesson at another time might connect the dots in a way that it did not before. This is why the 'beginner's mind' is so helpful. Instead of completely writing something off you are open to the possibility, that at another time or place, it could help you in a way that you could not have previously anticipated.

The key to learning from others is to understand that what has worked for them (or the examples they provide) may, or may not, be applicable to you. Be open to hearing and seeing what might be possible, but continually filter the information for what is most relevant. Ensure that you stay true to what is best for you. If you do not, you can end up bouncing from one person's idea to the next. If you are not careful then you might lose all sense of what your game is all about. Your game is unique to you. Whatever you take from others must be coherent with the way that you are.

The mistakes that you make are an opportunity. They are not the first errors you have made, and neither will they be the last. Get comfortable with making errors. Laugh at them and then learn from them. If you could have done better, you would have done. Now that you know, you can do the work that the next step requires.

Without continual learning, success eventually comes to an end. Mastery is about valuing the journey as much as it is about achieving your goals. Enjoy the process from where you are - both physically in time and given your current skillset. Do not be too drawn in by your highest ambitions - instead be engrossed with what you can do right now. Be who you are and do it your own way. There is *always* more to learn, no matter how good you are or what you already know. Keep looking for answers and you will find them.

What are the most valuable lessons that you have learned about the game?

Have there been occasions when your expectations or judgments have got in the way of learning?

Mastery requires you to find out what it will take to be successful. Not just wishing for it, but to understand everything that is required on and off the field. To know what you need to do to succeed and to keep learning from victories and defeats. To identify what delivers high performance in your field. Consider not only the obvious, standout components, but also the small gains that when added up and applied regularly can make a big difference.

Be honest about where your game is at. Only when you fully understand what it takes, will 'The Work' become transformative. Let go of any excuses and see your game exactly as it is - great in places, but not so good or a work in progress in other areas.

The 'Pareto Principle' suggests that 80% of results are created by 20% of the input.

Do you know what makes up the 20% - i.e. what really matters - that determines most of your results?

What will you have to do today, tomorrow and the next day to learn, improve and perform?

What is needed to be successful at this level, the next one and the one after that?

Anyone can talk a good game but, to realise your potential, you need to spend the necessary time practicing and refining your skills to master your craft. The most skilled people on the planet have spent thousands of hours developing their abilities. This is so much easier to do if you love the game and do not define yourself by the results. Then practice becomes as much fun as competition, and can be just as challenging.

Doing 'The Work' is a process of trial and error. The goal is to craft your unique skillset and know how to apply it to the situations that you will encounter.

Does it matter what anybody else says if you find for yourself what truly works for you?

Progress is not going to be linear. Your ego wants progress to be straightforward, for you to 'tick all the boxes' and become an 'overnight success' story. However, if this did happen, it would make playing the game pointless. The occasions when reality does not match your hopes and expectations are what provides the opportunity for you to grow.

The more on the edge of your comfort zone (technically, tactically, physically and mentally) that your practice is, the more progress you will make. The time spent honing your skills can be chaotic. Sometimes you have to go down one road only to find out that a better one exists, or that you were better off sticking with where you were in the first place. This is all part of the process. It is OK to get it wrong and it is OK to temporarily get a little lost as you attempt to move forwards.

Practice sessions should move between being representative of the complexity of matches and being simplified for learning something new or for repetition of skills. Conditions that are most like how they will be in matches will enable you to develop all aspects of your game that will be tested in competition. Simplifying the environment allows for sufficient grooving of the movements that make up a skill. Practice should also shift between sessions being an experiment and opportunity for exploration and time spent on fundamentals and preparation.

Find out what works, and what does not. Then, adjust and go again. This path never ends and the chance to learn never ceases. There is no substitute for learning from your own experiences.

Be clear on what you are trying to work on, regardless of whether you are in good or bad 'form'. Otherwise it becomes tempting to search for quick fixes which tend to create more problems than they solve. While you should learn from what has happened in recent matches, stick with a clear process of developing your game and do not get thrown off track just because it has not gone to plan recently.

High performance is 'instinctive competence' - being

skilled and having faith in your instincts knowing what to do. When you are learning, there is often an analytical thinking process that helps you to figure out the challenge. This enables you to identify what you are working on and how the skill may look, or feel, differently to get the best possible outcome. Then, allow your instincts to take over again once you have got a feel for the movement.

Just as effective performance does, effective practice must find a balance of ebb and flow between instinct and intellect. The more aware of what you are doing that you become, without getting caught up in judging it as 'good' or 'bad', the more feedback that you will get. You will come to understand your game with more clarity and uncover the blind spots.

A natural process of change can take place where technique improves through awareness and adjustment. Alternatively, you only end up getting in your way when you attempt to improve your skills with an overuse of analysis, conscious thinking and judgment. The key to skill acquisition is 'feel' and intuition. When learning becomes natural again, you find the method that feels and works best for you at your stage of development.

> *"Even though we have the ability to learn*
> *naturally, many of us have forgotten.*
> *And many of us have lost touch with feel.*
> *We may need to learn how to feel again*
> *and learn how to learn again. Remember*
> *that you are not tennis game. You are not*
> *your body. Trust the body to learn and to*
> *play, as you would trust another person*
> *to do a job" - Tim Galwey*

'The Work' is more effective when you love what you are doing so that time spent crafting your skills feels engaging rather than a chore. Practice because *you want* to practice. Show up day in, day out and do your best. Push yourself as far as you can on the given day. Raise the standards of what you do. However, 'your best' will vary. Some days will feel better than others. 'Your best' should be defined by how you got the most out of practice, considering how you felt and what you were capable of on the day. This differs vastly from perfection. Perfection is an unattainable standard, a concept that you search for when you feel insecure. Trying to fix that insecurity with a 'perfect' performance will only end up in 'beating yourself up' when you inevitably do not reach it.

It is liberating to understand that what might look like perfection from the outside will probably not feel like perfection to you at the time. It feels like the best you can do, and on that day, everything just finds a way of working out. Having any higher standards of yourself than that is setting yourself up to fail. All that you can do is your best.

Over time, turning up again and again and doing 'The Work' as best you can leads to a level of performance that is always a lot better than when you started. Whatever you spend your time and attention on is going to improve. Identify what matters and give it the time and attention it deserves.

> *"Change starts here or not at all.*
> *Concrete, humble steps are best. Small is*
> *good. Over and over is good. It will lead*
> *to remarkable progress." - Steven Hayes*

Too often we overcomplicate 'The Work' believing it to be

more than this. This overcomplication leads to judgments about perceived progress that then become the barrier to improving. Instead, keeping it simple - committing time and attention to 'The Work' - enables you to see things as they are without labelling or judging it. This is the foundation of all improvement.

Commitment gives you the patience to handle difficult times and low points, as well as enjoying the highs. It simplifies doing 'The Work' and makes it less of an effort and a grind. Commitment means that you will keep doing 'The Work', even at times when you do not feel like it or you are experiencing doubts or insecurities. There becomes a distinction between how you feel about the game temporarily, and a deeper sense to persevere.

An unconditional commitment comes from the love of the game. It fuels a continuous drive to improve. No matter what happened before, you keep taking your game forward. When you have this love of, and commitment to, the game, you will always practice *enough*. It becomes a case of working smart and focusing on the quality of your practice, rather than just putting in the hours for the sake of it.

Do you know how much practice is right for you?

What types of practice do you utilise and why?

Commitment frees you from ruminating on alternatives - people, places or results. If you are in one place and thinking of another, you suffer the experience of not being truly in either place. Commitment makes sure that it is only the 'here and now' that matters.

SUCCESS AND FAILURE

"If you can meet triumph and disaster; And treat those two imposters both the same."

Rudyard Kipling

Failure is one way of looking at an inherently neutral situation for a moment in time. There is always another way of looking at it. What feels like a failure to one person, does not to another. It is likely that you will look back at the same moment or event completely differently some time from now. With hindsight, most of what you thought were failures were blessings in disguise. Without something going wrong, there would have been no opportunity to learn. However, because feeling that you have failed can be uncomfortable, it can be tempting to give up the process to avoid those feelings.

There is no right or wrong way to respond to a perceived failure. You might be 'as calm as a cucumber' or completely devastated. Either way, you must learn from what happened and move on from the experience. There is no value in trying to hold on to the past or wishing that things had been different. They are exactly what they are. Your only task is to take what you can from the situation and then let it go. Resentment about what happened just makes you feel bitter.

Make peace with the knowledge that you will 'lose it'

occasionally. Which is to say that you will get lost in your thinking, and temporarily not see the situation clearly, and act in a way that makes sense given that lack of clarity. By being OK with 'losing it', any habit of doing so begins to fade away of its own accord. This is because your thinking does not spiral into judgment about how you, or others, should be seeing things or acting differently. When it happens, it happens. It stops being a big deal, and when it is not a big deal, you no longer get caught in the habit of 'losing it' very often. Everybody reacts differently to a bad day; do not take it personally, learn from it and move on.

If you view your mistakes as a genuine problem, rather than as something that can be learned from, you are going to get stuck quickly. Avoid identifying with your game as if it is actually who you are. Otherwise, you lose all sense of perspective. You will make excuses and statements like "I don't care anyway!" when you make errors. This is a defence mechanism of the ego. An excuse that tries to protect the self-image that has got wrapped up in results and outcomes.

If you genuinely do not care, then that is fair enough. However, it is likely that making an excuse is an example of the fact that you *do* care. You would not go to the effort of making an excuse otherwise. The freedom is in knowing that you are OK whether you win or lose, because your sense of identity is founded on who you really are, and not what your mind wants other people to think of you.

Experiencing doubts is OK. As thoughts and feelings fluctuate, doubt is inevitable. A doubt is sometimes exactly what you need. You have the thought "I am not good enough" and it gives you the opportunity to explore it. You can identify exactly what you need to do to become sufficiently skilled. Alternatively, it teaches you the lesson that not all thoughts need to be believed.

You can explore uncomfortable thoughts for the grain of truth in them, or to see that you do not need to hold on to them. Rather than resisting these thoughts, understanding them for what they are takes the energy out of them. Doubts will then flow through naturally, rather than you becoming fixated on them. If the next thought is judgmental, just know that it is a thought. You do not have to do anything with it.

Whatever you believe success to be, you need failure in equal measure. Failure is the anchor that defines success. You only understand success in relation to failure. Whatever you believe failure to be matters because it provides your opportunity for learning and improvement. Failure is the road to you growing, as a player and as a person. When you do not match up to your expectations, or someone else's that you believe defines success, then it will feel like 'failure'. These experiences create the chance for you to assess what is working and what is not, and to go again, wiser for having failed.

When you seek to protect your sense of self through excuses or by stopping playing the game altogether, you miss the opportunity to learn and therefore to fully realise your potential. This is because you do not want to feel like a failure. However, you can judge results too quickly. If you put too much attention on the immediate consequences, you might miss seeing the bigger picture. The game is always going to be full of ups and downs. Failure is neither a fixed entity nor the final stop on your journey.

The desire not to fail can become a 'fear of failure'. Rather than stretching yourself and seeing the tough days as an essential part of the whole, you tense up and grind away to be 'good enough' - to be slightly better than what you define failure to be. This can mean that you do 'enough' but never unearth your full potential because, as soon as you have ensured that you have not failed, there is no drive to keep going. You have done 'enough' and believe "that will do".

You will lose matches. However, you do not fundamentally lose anything by being defeated. You are not less of a person. You are not reliant on the result. You do not have to prove yourself. These are all beliefs that have looked real for so long that you have forgotten that they are solely thoughts and not truths.

With this understanding, fear of failure ceases to exist. You have seen through the illusion. There is nothing to lose, so there is no true failure. There is nothing to fear. Even if you lose everything, you are *still* OK. Let go of the belief that the game can give you something that you *need*. When you are no longer constrained by fearful illusions, success becomes far simpler to achieve.

Performers often play at their best when they feel that they have 'nothing to lose'. They might get this sense when nothing else has worked and they feel that they are in a 'last chance saloon'. Then they relax, and go out and enjoy it as they know that it might be their last match (e.g. for that team, at that level or even, ever). This feeling of freedom helps their game click back into place. However, having played so freely and successfully, they then usually forget the 'nothing to lose' perspective and slip back into the belief of *needing* to play well. They tense up again and become less than the player that they were when they just *let go*.

The truth is that there really is nothing to lose. Except what you think there is.

How freeing is that?

Resilience is far simpler than you might think. From the outside, what looks like resilience, 'mental toughness', 'bouncebackability' and persistence looks very hard to achieve. If you are playing the game to prove yourself rather than to enjoy the game, then bouncing back *will be* more effortful. The lows will be lower because, not only do you have to move on from what has happened, but you also have to let go of what you think it says about you. However, resilience is a natural process when you love what you are doing and do not hold onto any insecure thoughts about your results.

Everyone wants to deliver their best performances more often. Aiming for consistency, however, is a 'fool's errand'. Consistency is not something that can be successfully attained by striving for it. Instead, it is a description of performances that have already taken place. 'Form' is what the past looks like on a piece of paper.

You cannot become a better performer by aiming for something (a sequence of outcomes) that exists only in the past (your last result) and the future (your next result). By bringing the past into the present, it takes you out of where your attention needs to be.

The more consistent you attempt to become, the more inconsistent your results are likely to be. You are not consistent. You are not exactly the same person (physically or psychologically) from one day to the next.

The desire for consistency only creates an inner resistance to the reality of your performances. This impedes further progress because, on top of the inherent challenges of the game, you have added another layer of thinking to deal with. A focus on future performances, through the desire for consistency, only takes your attention away from the only place that results are created: Now.

Being able to adapt from where you are is more valuable than striving for the notion of consistency. You can only do what you can do right now, in the present. Sometimes the momentum of the game seems to be going with you and at others it does not. Playing your best requires working with both. You do not know how it is going to end up. You have to surrender to the unknown and patiently find out.

If you are not achieving the results that you are aiming for, consider what needs more time and attention - your skills and/or your understanding of yourself and the game. Your experience, your game and your results are all better when you relax into them. If you are in great rhythm do not think about it, just do it. Rather than getting caught up in the concepts of consistency and form, or comparing yourselves to others, just allow the game to flow from where you are. Explore what is possible, work with each moment as it arises and have fun finding out what happens.

PBP KEY #3 PLAY YOUR GAME: SUMMARY

1. Assume that you *are* instinct, and that everything you learn is a layer on top of what comes naturally. Sometimes the layers of beliefs and thinking need to be stripped back.

2. 'Choking' and 'The Yips' are what happens when instinctive movements are hijacked by conscious, analytical thinking.

3. Play *This* Ball. While the intellect can help you analyse and prepare, then let go and allow instinct to take over. Trusting your instincts is trusting yourself.

4. Concentration is natural and inevitable if you are enjoying what you are doing. You can only ever be distracted by your own thoughts.

5. Your 'Adapted Method' is your way of playing the game - your talents and learned skills, strengths and weaknesses - combined with playing the role required

given the demands of the circumstances.

6. 'Being comfortable feeling uncomfortable' comes from knowing that you are OK no matter what happens and that while insecure thoughts will always come and go, you do not have to buy into them.

7. The search for confidence only gets in the way of experiencing it. All feelings, including confidence, will ebb and flow. You do not *need* to feel confident.

8. Mastery is the process of continual learning and commitment to refining your craft. Failure is just a perception designed to help you learn.

9. It is more valuable to gain a clear 'feel' for what you are doing, and trying to achieve, than it is to describe it intellectually.

10. Form is what the past looks like on a piece of paper. What matters most is what you do, right now, in the present.

PLAY BEYOND PRESSURE

"To play is to yield oneself to a kind of magic. In play, the mind is prepared to accept the unimagined and incredible, to enter a world where different laws apply, to be relieved all of weights that bear it down.
To be free."

Hugo Rahner

It is possible to become so focused on performance that you forget to play. When you forget to play, you get tense and do not perform. The difference between performance and play is how it feels. Performance feels heavy and a burden. Play feels light and a fun experience.

Play is a way of being. The game is still fundamentally the same, but your approach to it can get in the way of playing it with freedom. Play is open and flexible; it is without fixed ideas or rigid plans. There are no expectations, and you are ready for anything. Play is openness to the game's possibilities and a fearlessness to meet the unknown.

How much fun might it be to realise that this is all *play?*

What a weight off your shoulders it is to know that *playing* the game is infinitely more valuable than *performing* at it. The spirit of the game is different when you are playing the game, rather than performing at it or using it as a tool for self-validation. This enables you to have a deeper respect for your opponent and the officials, stemming from a deeper understanding of yourself and the game. You go back to the simplicity of enjoying the game and challenging yourself to the edge of your skills and abilities.

The more that you love the game, the more fun it becomes. Therefore, you spend more time playing and practicing, and so the better you become. This is a virtuous cycle - the more you give, the more that you get back. Saying that you love the game can make the ego feel vulnerable and insecure because its sense of validation is attached to the outcome. However, it is by moving beyond this limited sense of identity that you can experience the unlimited connection with, and unconditional satisfaction from, playing the game. This frees you up to express yourself on the field. You become more motivated, but without any weight on your shoulders. You know that there is nothing to prove.

Your journey, both in the game and away from the field of play, is uniquely your own. There will always be opinions, judgments, comparisons and help from others. However, it is learning about yourself and the game, for yourself, that is endlessly rewarding. This is a ceaseless path of realising your potential - ball by ball, moment by moment, game by game. Every match, opponent, situation, success and failure will ask a different question of you. In the end the only game worth playing is the one where you know that it *is* a game, and you are *playing* it.

What might be possible if you were to *play* on the biggest stage rather than perform on it?

Can you treat the 'biggest' match as a backyard game?

Because, without all your thinking about it, that is what it is.

> *"This is the real secret of life - to be completely engaged with what you are doing in the here and now. And instead of calling it work, realise it is play."*
> *- Alan Watts*

Realising your potential is as much an inner journey as an outer one. It comes from continually going beyond your perceived limits. You become fully aware of the two games – inner and outer – that are taking place and the dynamics at play within each of them. You go beyond your perceptions every time that you insightfully have a deeper perspective on what is happening. This occurs when you view each situation exactly as it is, see what might be possible and let go of the old perspective that was holding you back. All of this takes place instinctively - insightfully - when you know that this is the natural learning process.

When you understand each of the keys - yourself, the game and your game - you will see that they are all intertwined.

Your perspective on and ability to play the game grows through understanding yourself. The game helps you to learn more about who you are, how to get better and why you react to the world in the way that you do. As you understand yourself and the game with increased clarity, creating results becomes enjoyable and exciting, as stress and insecurity fall way. By finding what works for you, you create *your* game and see how you can 'be yourself' *and* achieve results.

Sometimes it feels like you are making it happen. And when it does, go with it and keep making it happen. However, if you look closely enough, this is all taking place by itself. There is a power behind life, and it is rolling forward with or without what you think. You are one particle of this infinite energy, in an infinite sequence of events and endless opportunities, flowing through time and space. You are not in as much control as you might have thought, but it is this realisation that creates inner liberation.

This realisation means that you can go with the ebb and flow of the game, knowing that underneath it all you are always OK. Nothing that happens can define you. All the tension of "I must achieve this" and "I must be *this* person" evaporates. The reality is that, whether you want it to or not, it will either happen or it will not. Your role is to enjoy finding out and then move forward, leaving the past in the past.

Keep showing up, giving it everything and loving what you do. Embrace uncertainty and the unknown - you are guaranteed to find them at every turn. You can always go further than you thought possible. Every problem is an opportunity for you to go beyond, as you see that there are no inherent, pre-defined problems; only neutral situations that you experience temporary, illusory thoughts about and can accidentally, but unhelpfully, begin to derive your sense of identity from.

Trust your instincts - you have your own best answers. Often, the best solutions are far simpler than you might realise. The purpose of taking your own path is to have your own insights and your own, wide-open perspective on what happens both in the game and beyond. The more deeply that you understand yourself and the game, the more insightful experiences that you will have.

"The solution to outwardly complex problems created by misguided thought will not arise from complicated analytical theory, but will emerge as an insight wrapped in a blanket of simplicity."
- Sydney Banks

The moment that you realise that your reality is created by thought, you have the chance to see beyond it. Look beyond what you think, perceive, and feel. Let go of expectation and judgment. Everything that happens to you is inherently neither good nor bad. It is what it is, and you are where you are.

Pressure is an 'outside-in' illusion. It is a temporary perception, based on who you believe that you are and how you think that the game of life works. You are always able to go beyond an illusion once you know that it is all it is. Beyond the illusion is the infinite space of consciousness, the awareness within which everything internal and external arises. To go beyond is to go back home - to base camp. You come back to yourself.

This understanding leaves you with the clarity to be fully engaged with the here and now. Deal with *this* moment, learn and then let it go. Be grounded to reality and not any fiction that the mind can create. This simple reality is far more magical than any ingrained pattern of thinking can imagine. The less that you get tangled up in thoughts, and the more that you see yourself as beyond what you think, the more fulfilled and effective that you become.

In the absence of believing illusory thoughts and beyond the constraints of your self-image, you feel connected to everything - the game, the ball, the opponent, the crowd. All these elements merge into one. Here, you become immersed in all that matters - the present moment.

There, you are not under pressure, but beyond it, whether you experience the feeling or not. With that knowledge, you fully express yourself. It is here that ordinary people become capable of extraordinary things.

"You were born to be a player. You were meant to be here. This moment is yours."

Herb Brooks

ABOUT THE AUTHOR

 Rich Hudson is Managing Director of Buckinghamshire Cricket and a Well-Being & Performance consultant.

Perform Beyond Pressure is Rich's second book, after *Pressure Myths* was published in 2018.

He is an England & Wales Cricket Board Level 4 'Master Coach', with a Post-Graduate Diploma in Elite Cricket Coaching and a Master of Science degree in Sport Psychology. Rich lives in Northampton, England, with his wife Rachel.

If you are interested in finding out more Rich's work or would like to contact him, please visit his website *www.rdh00.co.uk* or follow on Twitter @rdhudson00

For 10% off Rich's online courses, use the coupon code: PBPbook when signing up at https://rdh00.teachable.com

ACKNOWLEDGMENTS

My thanks and appreciation go to:

My wife, Rachel, and father, Brian, for all their help with the edit.

Fran Wilson, Josh Poysden, Luke Swann, Nathan Wood, Sam Jarman and Toby Bailey for the discussions that are part of the *Performing Beyond Pressure* online course (*https://rdh00.teachable.com*).

www.tealzebra.co.uk for the cover design.